How Institutions Think

The Frank W. Abrams Lectures

THE FRANK W. ABRAMS LECTURES

Supported by a grant from the Exxon Educational Foundation and published by Syracuse University Press

Stanley Hoffmann. *Duties Beyond Borders: On the Limits and Possibilities of Ethical International Politics.* 1981.

James C. Coleman. *The Asymmetric Society.* 1982.

Guido Calabresi. *Ideals, Beliefs, Attitudes, and the Law.* 1985.

Robert Dahl. *Controlling Nuclear Weapons: Democracy versus Guardianship.* 1985.

Mary Douglas. *How Institutions Think.* 1986.

How Institutions

Think

MARY DOUGLAS

SYRACUSE UNIVERSITY PRESS 1986

The paper used in this publication meets the minimum requirements of American
National Standard for Information Sciences—Permanence of Paper for
Printed Library Materials, ANSI Z39.48-1984. ∞

Library of Congress Cataloging-in-Publication Data

Douglas, Mary Tew.
  How institutions think.

  (The Frank W. Abrams lectures)
  Bibliography: p.
  Includes index.
  1. Social institutions—Psychological aspects.
2. Cognition and culture. 3. Organizational behavior.
I. Title. II. Series.
GN479.D68 1986   306   86-5696
ISBN 0-8156-2369-0 (alk. paper)
ISBN 0-8156-0206-5 (pbk. : alk. paper)

Contents

MARY DOUGLAS earned her bachelor's, master's, and doctorate degrees from Oxford University. Early in her career, she did fieldwork in the Belgian Congo under the auspices of the International African Institute. She has been a lecturer in anthropology at Oxford and at University College of London, a reader in anthropology at the University of London and, later, professor of social anthropology there. In 1977 she came to America as Director for Research on Culture at the Russell Sage Foundation, and in 1981 she went to Northwestern University as Avalon Foundation Professor in the Humanities, and is currently Visiting Professor at Princeton University.

Foreword

MARY DOUGLAS presented the sixth Abrams Lectures at Syracuse University during the last two weeks of March 1985. The series is underwritten by a grant from the Exxon Education Foundation in memory of Frank W. Abrams, former Chairman of the Board of Standard Oil Company (New Jersey), the predecessor of Exxon, and a former Chairman of the Board of Trustees of Syracuse University.

Mr. Abrams was a life-long leader in the support of higher education. He founded the Council for Financial Aid to Education, served as chairman of the Ford Foundation's Fund for the Advancement of Education, and was a trustee of the Alfred E. Sloan Foundation. Mr. Abrams was instrumental in awakening American business both through education and through landmark legal precedents, to the special need for financial support by business of private higher education.

The Exxon Education Foundation continues to expand upon the early work of Frank Abrams. The Foundation's leadership role in the support of higher education is certainly well known and respected. We are grateful to the Foundation for its generous support of several University undertakings and particularly proud of the Abrams Lecture Series since Frank Abrams was a 1912 graduate of Syracuse University.

A special thank you is due the members of the Abrams Lecture Series Planning Committee, headed by Guthrie S. Birkhead,

vii

Dean of the Maxwell School of Citizenship and Public Affairs. Working with Dean Birkhead are Michael O. Sawyer, Vice Chancellor of the University and Professor of Constitutional Law; L. Richard Oliker, Dean of the School of Management; Richard D. Schwartz, Ernest I. White Professor of Law; Chris J. Witting, Chairman of the Syracuse University Board of Trustees; and Robert L. Payton, President of the Exxon Education Foundation.

Mary Douglas was a most accommodating lecturer and campus guest. She presented five impressive lectures, met regularly with faculty and graduate students, visited undergraduate classes, and brought her own special brand of sunshine to the sometimes bleak days of early Syracuse spring.

MELVIN A. EGGERS

Chancellor
Syracuse University

Preface

THIS BOOK is the result of an invitation by Syracuse University to give the sixth set of lectures in the Frank W. Abrams Series. In such a case, the theme is partly indicated by the form of the occasion. A charge from the Maxwell School of Citizenship and Public Affairs requires some large topic. An invitation to lecture requires that the topic be packed into a small space. To have been chosen as the lecturer suggested that a personal synthesis would be appropriate. It appeared irresistibly as a chance to say again what I have already tried to say. Speaking this time to the attentive, critical audience from Syracuse University meant trying to put the theme in a new light, to make it clearer and more persuasive, and perhaps, at last, to say it right.

A theory of institutions that will amend the current unsociological view of human cognition is needed, and a cognitive theory to supplement the weaknesses of institutional analysis is needed as well. The theme is big enough, topical and untried enough for a speculative approach. This is the first book I should have written after writing on African fieldwork. Instead I wrote *Purity and Danger* (1966) in an attempt to generalize from Africa to our own condition. My friends told me at the time that *Purity and Danger* was obscure, intuitive, and ill-prepared. They were right, and I have been trying ever since to understand the theoretical and logical anchoring that I would have needed to present a coherent argument about the social control of cognition. This volume is one more *post hoc* introduction. It is like a prolegomenon to *Risk Acceptability* (1986), which points an accusing finger at professional blind spots and rooted resistance to the theme. *Risk Acceptability*, in its turn, is like an appended introduction to *Risk and Culture* (1982 with Aaron Wildavsky), a book which shows how the anthropological analysis of public beliefs can be extended to our own case. But *Risk and Culture* is the argument that should have been in place before *Implicit Meanings* was published in 1970 with an essay called "Environments at Risk." They should all have appeared in reverse order, ending with *The Lele of the Kasai* (1963). If that were the case, the Abrams Lecture Committee would now be receiving the first in the series. But how could that have happened, indebted as I have become over the long stretch of time? Many writers, young and old and some, alas, now dead, have helped me at each stage. I wish I could hope that this volume might be so acceptable as to break the spell, so that I could now start writing forwards instead of backwards.

This book begins with the hostility that greeted Emile Durkheim and the Durkheimians when they talked about institutions or social groups as if they were individuals. The very idea of a suprapersonal cognitive system stirs a deep sense of outrage. The offense taken in itself is evidence that above the level of the individual human another hierarchy of "individuals" is influencing lower-level members to react violently against this idea or that. An individual that encompasses thinking humans is assumed to be of a nasty totalitarian sort, a highly centralized and effective dictatorship. For example, Anthony Greenwald draws on Hannah Arendt and George Orwell for totalitarian models of what he calls extrapersonal knowledge domains (1980). Whereas reflection makes plain that, at higher levels of organization, controls over lower-level constituent members tend to be weaker and more diffuse. Many subtle and able thinkers are made so nervous by the crude political analogy between individual mind and social influences on cognition that they prefer to dismiss the whole problem.

Anthropologists cannot dismiss it. Emile Durkheim, E. Evans-Pritchard, and Claude Lévi-Strauss are great leaders to follow. The one scholar whose mark is most strongly on the whole area covered here is Robert Merton. To him I respectfully and affectionately dedicate the book, trusting his generosity to overlook its failings. My husband deserves a special tribute. When two problems seem insoluble, our long experience of domestic life has suggested an oblique approach. Instead of a head-on attack on each separate issue, one set of problems can be made to confront the other. This strategy, which produces new definitions of what has to be solved, gives the framework of this book.

Over two delightful weeks I enjoyed the warm hospitality of Chancellor and Mrs. Eggers and of many programs and departments at Syracuse. The work was lightened by the welcome and support of Guthrie Birkhead, Dean of the Maxwell School, by the wise counsel of Manfred Stanley (and I do not forget the steady constructive criticism from his family), and by the perfect organization of James G. Gies.

Different sections have been tried out in one form or another. Chapters one and two were presented at the Conference on Right Categories sponsored by the Wenner-Gren Foundation in honor of Nelson Goodman at Northwestern University in 1985, and I thank all the participants for this discussion. I thank Kai Erikson for the opportunity to rehearse parts of chapter three in the Hollingshead Memorial Lecture at Yale University. An early version of chapters six and seven was given in the panel on "Is Social Order Possible?" at the American Sociology Association meeting in San Antonio in 1983, and I thank the Chairman, James Shorter, for permission to publish this lengthier study of public memory. Part of chapter nine was given in Russell Hardin's seminar on ethics in the University of Chicago, and I thank Russell Hardin and Alan Gewirth for their helpful criticisms. David Bloor, Barry Barnes, and Lawrence Rosen have also given important criticisms. Many in Northwestern University have argued about and criticized different sections. Reid Hastie supplied a necessary balance and a pile of references from psychological writings. Robert Welsch read the whole manuscript and made helpful criticisms. Andrew Leslie worked on the bibliography. Richard Kerber researched the classifications of the wine trade. Helen McFaul has given the ideal kind of secretarial support that a writer may dream about, far beyond the call of duty.

MD

Introduction

WRITING ABOUT COOPERATION and solidarity means writing at the same time about rejection and mistrust. Solidarity involves individuals being ready to suffer on behalf of the larger group and their expecting other individual members to do as much for them. It is difficult to talk about these questions coolly. They touch on intimate feelings of loyalty and sacredness. Anyone who has accepted trust and demanded sacrifice or willingly given either knows the power of the social bond. Whether there is a commitment to authority or a hatred of tyranny or something between the extremes, the social bond itself is taken to be something above question. Attempts to bring it out into the light of day and to investigate it are resisted. Yet it needs to be examined. Everyone is affected directly by the quality of trust around him or her. Sometimes a gullible steadfastness allows leaders to ignore the public need. Sometimes trust is short term and fragile, dissolving easily into panic. Sometimes mistrust is so deep that cooperation is impossible.

A contemporary example will help to bring the abstract issues into focus. In the field of nuclear medicine there is a superb record of mutual trust and cooperation. The scientists have an acceptable means of checking each others' claims; they believe in their methods and have faith in the results in the same way as doctors and patients trust each other. If the strength of solidarity can be measured by the sheer power of achievements, we have here

1

a strong instance. Rosalyn Yalow has recently made a report (1985) on the history of the subdiscipline in which she has spent her professional life. Her report was inspired by signs that the work is now about to be stopped. It is under heavy attack due to fear of the ill effects of nuclear radiation. Nothing that the scientists can say in its defense can dispel the mistrust.

Rosalyn Yalow joined the Veterans Administration Hospital in the Bronx in the 1940s in order to establish a Radioisotope Service that would use radioactive tracers for investigating disease. Since then the achievements of the Service have been awe-inspiring. First doctors used radio iodine to investigate the physiology of the thyroid and to treat it. At the same time they used it to measure the volume of blood in circulation in the body. This enabled them to develop experimental methods for assessing the rates of synthesis and degradation of serum proteins in the blood. Applying these techniques to the turnover of insulin in the body led to a major revision of what had been known about diabetes. From successes in treating thyroid and diabetes, the work led to the principle of radioimmunoassay (RIA). This is a way of imaging physiological processes by administering radioisotopes to patients and tracing their behavior in the body. The applications of RIA are innumerable in all branches of medicine. It is used in statewide programs for detecting underactivity of thyroid glands in the newborn. This is a disorder not detectable by clinical methods that affects 1 in 4,000 births in the United States and 4 in 100 in the so-called goiter belt in the region south of the Himalayas. If it is not treated shortly after birth, it results in irreversible mental retardation. From detection and management of malignant cancer to heart disease, there seems to be no limit to the application of RIA.

On the other side of this impressive record in medicine, millions of people have been exposed to low doses of nuclear radiation and some hundreds of thousands to moderate doses. Evidence has accumulated to show that acute exposure to high doses can quickly be lethal, and that chronic exposure to more moderate doses can result in malignancies or early death. The present criticism that threatens the medical applications of RIA considers these dangers. How low is low? What is a short or long exposure? Is fear justified? These are questions that Rosalyn Yalow's report sets out to answer.

The subject is highly technical. From the dawn of humanity our forebears have been exposed to radiation from the natural radioactivity of soil and food and from extraterrestrial cosmic rays. These constitute the levels of natural background radiation, which vary from region to region. On average, medical radiation exposure adds an amount about equal to the natural background. To know whether this is dangerous to health it is easy to design research in regions of the world where natural background radiation is particularly high to see whether those exposed have higher cancer rates. In the United States, seven states have higher natural background radiation than the rest, but their cancer rate is lower than the mean cancer rate in the whole country. High altitude involves high radiation exposure, but in the United States an inverse relationship is reported between elevation and leukemias and lymphomas. A careful study in China examined 150,000 Han peasants with essentially similar lifestyle and genetic makeup. Half of them lived in a region of radioactive soil where they received almost threefold higher exposure than the other half. The research evaluated a large number of possible radiation effects on health but failed to find any difference between the inhabitants of the two areas. So these and other investigations point to the conclusion that radiation exposure at three or even ten times the natural background does not affect health adversely.

This volume is not concerned with whether what Yalow calls "a phobic fear of radiation" is right or wrong. The example illuminates several other points that are at issue in the pages that follow. The bitter disagreement between the scientists practicing nuclear medicine on the one hand and a section of the general public on the other illustrates the selective deafness in which neither of two parties to a debate can hear what the other is saying. Later chapters will attribute the inability to be converted by reasoned argument to the hold that institutions have on our processes of classifying and recognizing. The nuclear medics are saying that they are not taking chances with their patients' lives or exposing the rest of the population to danger. The nuclear phobics are denying this because they know that all medicine entails risk. To brush it aside would be dishonest. Medical knowledge and skill can never be sufficient. Having rejected the claim that no danger is involved, some of their interest focuses on the trade-off between the sick who have been saved and the whole population that has been endangered: no one has the right to decide who shall be sacrificed for the good of others. In riposte, it is argued that the nuclear phobics are arrogating to themselves just such a decision, since they are putting the rights of the healthy before the lives of cancer victims, diabetics, thyroid and heart cases, and newborn babies about to be mentally retarded, who would be saved by the powerful new diagnostic techniques and treatment. The strategic answer is to decline the honor of choosing between sacrificial victims: this involves insisting that alternative medicine and good diet would improve our life chances just as well as nuclear medicine, if only they were given an equal chance.

The debate between the nuclear medics and the nuclear phobics gives the quintessential case for and against solidarity, expressed in an acute contemporary form. For solidarity is only gesturing when it involves no sacrifice. The last chapter will reconsider similar choices. To prepare for it, the preceding chapters will insist laboriously on the shared basis of knowledge and moral standards. The conclusion will be that individuals in crises do not make life and death decisions on their own. Who shall be saved and who shall die is settled by institutions. Putting it even more strongly, individual ratiocination cannot solve such problems. An answer is only seen to be the right one if it sustains the institutional thinking that is already in the minds of individuals as they try to decide.

A fictive example, "The Case of the Speluncean Explorers," was devised to illustrate precisely philosophers' divergent answers to the problem of whether one should be sacrificed for the lives of the others (Fuller 1949). The story is set in the Supreme Court of a place called Newgarth in the future year 4300. Four men have been convicted of homicide in a lower court and their case has come to the Supreme Court on appeal. The chief justice summarizes their story. Five members of the Speluncean Society set out to explore a deep cave; a fall of rock completely blocked the only entrance; a large rescue party started to tunnel through the rock, but the work was heavy and dangerous. Ten workmen were killed in the rescue attempt. On the twentieth day of their imprisonment radio contact was established and the trapped men asked how long it would take to free them. Another ten days were estimated as the minimum necessary. They asked for medical advice on the sufficiency of their rations and learned that they could not hope to survive for ten days more. They then asked if they could hope to survive if they consumed the flesh of one of their party and were told, reluctantly, that they could, but no one—priest or physician or philosopher— was willing to advise them on what to do. After that radio communication ceased. On the thirty-second day of their entombment the blocked entrance was pierced and four men walked out.

They said that one of them, Roger Whetmore, had proposed the solution of eating the flesh of one of the party, had suggested the choice be made by throwing dice, and produced a die that he happened to have with him. The others eventually agreed and were about to put the plan into action when he, Roger Whetmore, withdrew, saying that he preferred to wait another week. However, they went ahead, made his throw on his behalf, and, he then being indicated as the victim, they killed and ate him.

Opening the discussion, the chief justice expressed his opinion that the jury that had declared them guilty had acted correctly, since under the law there was no doubt about the facts; they had willfully taken the life of another. He proposed that the Supreme Court affirm the conviction and request clemency from the chief executive. Then followed the statements of the other four judges.

The first said it would be iniquitous to convict these men of murder: instead of a request for clemency he proposed they be acquitted. His argument invoked two separate principles. The trapped men had been removed geographically from the force of law; separated by a solid curtain of rock, they might as well have been on a desert island in a foreign territory. In desperate circumstances they were morally and legally in a state of nature, and the only law they were subject to was the charter or contract they made among themselves. Since ten workmens' lives had been sacrificed to save them, anyone who wished to convict the defendants should be prepared to prosecute the rescue organizations for murdering the workmen. Finally he drew upon the difference between the letter of the law and the interpretation of its purpose: it was no part of the purpose of the law defining homicide to condemn these starving men who could be said to have acted in self-defense.

The next judge disagreed vehemently with this argument, asking, "By what authority do we resolve ourselves into a Court of Nature?" He then withdrew from the decision.

The third judge also disagreed with the first, insisting that all the facts showed that the defendants did willfully take the life of their fellow. But he also disagreed with the chief justice's suggestion of a request for clemency. It was not proper for the judiciary to remake the law or to interfere with the other departments of government.

The last judge concluded that the defendants were innocent, not with any reference to the facts or the law, but because "men are ruled, not by words on paper or by abstract theories, but by other men": in this case the opinion polls showed that 90 percent of the public were in favor of clemency. However, he did not support the chief justice's recommendation because he knew that the chief executive, left to himself, would refuse to pardon and would be even more disinclined to clemency if a recommendation to that effect came from the Supreme Court: therefore he made no recommendation to pardon, but favored an acquittal.

Only the chief justice was in favor of asking for clemency. Two judges favored acquittal; two favored affirming the conviction; one withdrew. The Supreme Court being equally divided, the conviction in the lower court was affirmed, and the men were convicted and condemned to die by hanging.

In spinning this fable Lon Fuller has presented the standard range of judicial opinion from the Age of Pericles to the time of writing. Two of his judges feel strong sympathy for the defendants and recommend reversing the conviction, but on different grounds. The first judge evidently does not care for statutes at all (as one of his learned brothers complains). He is personally attracted by the idea of a state of nature, limited only by contract between individuals. He speaks movingly, as if he could envisage himself in the cave, making the compact and gambling on winning or losing all. His liberal views are appropriate to a form of society in which his risk-taking penchant and his readiness to negotiate would pay off. So congenial to him is the idea of contract that he overlooks the fact that the victim had withdrawn himself from it, and in proposing the argument of self-defense he even overlooks the other fact that the victim had posed no threat to the lives of the defendants. His fellow judges have no difficulty in finding grounds for disagreeing with him.

The last judge, who also recommended acquittal, hardly seems to be thinking like a lawyer at all. He wants to sweep away the silly legalities. He feels he can read the minds of the defendants and considers it would be outrageous to convict them after all the horrors they have endured. Motives and emotions are what matter to him. He also reads the mind of the chief executive, with whom he has family ties. The course he proposes is designed precisely to circumvent the bad motives of the chief executive. This wily and good-natured judge honors emotional truth. His stand corresponds to the views expressed in egalitarian sects that have been founded in order to reject pointless ritualism and to preach direct to men's hearts.

The third judge is neither sympathetic nor unsympathetic. The important things for him are the law, the judges' responsibilities in administering it, and the existing allocation of different functions within a complex state. He is a constitutionalist, at home in a hierarchical society.

The three judgments express three distinctive philosophies of law. It is no accident that Lon Fuller has picked on recurring themes in the history of jurisprudence. The themes recur because they correspond to forms of social life that recur. We have elsewhere described them as individualist, sectarian, and hierarchical (Douglas and Wildavsky 1982). Nothing will ever make those judges agree in a tangled matter of life and death. They are using their institutional commitments for thinking with. This book is written precisely to encourage more probing into the relation between minds and institutions.

To focus further on elementary principles of solidarity and trust, let us return to the story at the point where the five men learn that they will not survive on the food they have with them. They might have been a tourist party from a small and solidary village. Let us suppose that they shared the last judge's commitment to hierarchical principals. Then they would accept the idea that one of their number could rightfully be sacrificed for the survival of the others. The idea of choosing the victim by a game of dice would seem irrational and irresponsible. The leader would first take all responsibility and propose himself for the honor of sacrifice. Since the leader has some important role at home, the others would demur. Never could they emerge into the light of day, having killed and eaten the squire or the parish priest or the scout leader. Then the youngest and least important member would propose himself; the others would demur because of his youth and his life lying ahead. Then it would be the turn of the eldest, on the grounds that his life was over, and then the turn of the father of a large family. Throughout the last ten days of their captivity they would spend their time gently seeking a satisfactory hierarchical principle that would designate their victim, but they might never find one.

Now let us suppose that the prisoners in the cave are the members of a religious sect enjoying a holiday together. When they learn that 500 tons of rock have blocked their exit they rejoice, because they realize that the day of judgment has come and that they have been sealed away from Armageddon for their eternal salvation. So they pass their time of waiting in singing hymns of praise.

Only the individualists, bound by no ties to one another and imbued by no principles of solidarity, would hit upon the cannibal gamble as the proper course.

Arguing from different premises, we can never improve our understanding unless we examine and reformulate our assumptions. The following chapters are intended to clarify the extent to which thinking depends upon institutions. A clear framework is needed for a complex argument. I have chosen to approach solidarity and cooperation through the work of Emile Durkheim and Ludwik Fleck. For them, true solidarity is only possible to the extent that individuals share the categories of their thought. That such sharing is possible is unacceptable to many philosophers. It contradicts the basic axioms of the theory of rational behavior by which each thinker is treated as a sovereign individual. But the theory of rational choice, developed on this axiomatic structure, has insuperable difficulties with the idea of solidarity. The plan of these lectures was to bring the two approaches together, advocating that the ideas of Durkheim and Fleck be taken more seriously than heretofore in the discussions about the nature of the social bond. There is a tendency to dismiss Durkheim and Fleck because they seem to be saying that institutions have minds of their own. Of course institutions cannot have minds. It is worth spending time understanding what these thinkers really said.

1

Institutions Cannot Have Minds of Their Own

NOT JUST ANY BUSLOAD or haphazard crowd of people deserves the name of society: there has to be some thinking and feeling alike among members. But this is not to say that a corporate group possesses attitudes of its own. If it possesses anything, it is because of the legal theory that endows it with fictive personality. Yet, legal existence is not enough. Legal presumptions do not attribute emotional bias to corporations. Just because it is legally constituted, a group cannot be said to "behave"—still less to think or feel.

If this is literally true, it is implicitly denied by much of social thought. Marxist theory assumes that a social class can perceive, choose, and act upon its own group interests. Democratic theory is based on the idea of the collective will. Yet, when it comes to the detailed analysis, the theory of individual rational choice finds nothing but difficulties in the notion of collective behavior. It is axiomatic for the theory that rational behavior is based on self-regarding motives. The individual calculates what is in his best interest and acts accordingly. This is the basis of the theory on which economic analysis and political theory are based, and yet we get the contrary impression. Our intuition is that individuals do contribute to the public good generously, even unhesitatingly, without obvious self-serving. Whittling down the meaning of self-serving behavior until every possible disinterested motive is included merely makes the theory vacuous.

9

Emile Durkheim had another way of thinking about the conflict between individual and society (Durkheim 1903, 1912). He transferred it to warring elements within the person. For him the initial error is to deny the social origins of individual thought. Classifications, logical operations, and guiding metaphors are given to the individual by society. Above all, the sense of a priori rightness of some ideas and the nonsensicality of others are handed out as part of the social environment. He thought the reaction of outrage when entrenched judgments are challenged is a gut response directly due to commitment to a social group. In his view, the only program of research that would explain how a collective good is created would be work in epistemology.

Durkheim's thought is very apposite at this time. He believed that utilitarianism could never account for the foundations of civil society. Many of the sophisticated problems and paradoxes of utilitarianism were unsuspected in his day. But he was convinced all along that the Benthamite model, by which a social order is produced automatically out of the self-interested actions of rational individuals, was too limited because it gave no explanation of group solidarity.

Durkheim's sociological epistemology ran into considerable opposition and has remained undeveloped to this day. By upgrading the role of society in organizing thought, he downgraded the role of the individual. For this he was attacked as a rationalist and a radical. Since he did not spell out the precise steps of his functionalist argument, he attracted the opposite complaint—as being not too rational but appealing to irrationalism. He seemed to be invoking some mystic entity, the social group, and endowing it with superorganic, self-sustaining powers. For this he earned attack as a conservative social theorist. In spite of these weaknesses, his idea was still too good to be dismissed. Epistemological resources may be able to explain what cannot be explained by the theory of rational behavior.

According to Robert Merton, the French interest in the sociology of knowledge was largely independent of the prolific discussions of ideology and social consciousness conducted in Germany at the same time. Merton's essay on Karl Mannheim is essential background for this topic (1949). He pointed out that the French in their choice of problems emphasized "the range of variation among different peoples, not only of moral and social structures but of cognitive orientation as well." On the other hand, the

German sociology of knowledge was deeply marked by left-wing Hegelianism and by Marxist theory. In its early formulations, the sociology of knowledge in Germany was dogged by relativist problems and dominated by propagandist intentions. As these elements were gradually eliminated, the focus of the subject turned much more upon the relations of the individual to the social order in general. The effect of variation in the social order was (and is still) largely overlooked. All the focus was upon the interests. The usual typology of knowledge, for example, tends to explain different points of view by reference to the conflicting interests of different sections within modern industrial society. There was no attempt to compare viewpoints based on totally different types of society. Merton concludes his survey with a list of the logical flaws in Mannheim's arguments and exposes Mannheim's rhetorical devices for overcoming them. It is clear that no disciplined comparative framework would emerge from a sociology uninterested in the range of variety among different societies.

The French Durkheimian ideas have been less assimilated into the sociology of science by comparison with the German contribution. First, they were less compelling just because they were less political, dealing as they did with examples from distant, exotic peoples. Second, sociology, though it may have started with philosophical questions and political issues, received its major impulse for development because it provided an indispensable tool for administrative purposes. So Durkheim's intellectual program has languished.

Fortunately, the current wave of interest in Ludwik Fleck's work in the philosophy of science coincides with a wave of interest in political theory in the sources of commitment and altruism. In his book on the identification of syphilis, *The Genesis and Development of a Scientific Fact*, (1935), Fleck elaborated and extended Durkheim's approach. It would be worth making a detailed comparison of their points of agreement and their differences. In many places Fleck went far beyond Durkheim; in others he missed Durkheim's central synthesizing idea. Both were equally emphatic about the social basis of cognition.

In his skeptical attack on causal theories, David Hume had already posed the question for Durkheim; Hume had asserted that in our experience we only find succession and frequency, no laws or necessity. It is we ourselves who attribute causality.

Quoting Hume, Durkheim also posed the same question to an

imaginary audience of apriorist philosophers, defying them to show us "whence we hold this surprising prerogative and how it comes that we can see certain relations in things which the examination of these things cannot reveal to us." And his own answer was that the categories of time, space, and causality have a social origin.

> They represent the most general relations which exist between things; surpassing all our other ideas in extension, they dominate all the details of our intellectual life. If men do not agree upon these essential ideas at any moment, if they did not have the same conceptions of time, space, cause, number, etc., all contact between their minds would be impossible, and with that, all life together. Thus, society could not abandon the categories to the free choice of the individual without abandoning itself. . . . There is a minimum of logical conformity beyond which it cannot go. For this reason, it uses all its authority upon its members to forestall such dissidences. . . . The necessity with which the categories are imposed upon us is not the effect of simple habits whose yoke we can easily throw off with a little effort; nor is it a physical or metaphysical necessity, since the categories change in different places and times; it is a special sort of moral necessity which is to the intellectual life what moral obligation is to the will. (Durkheim 1912, pp. 29–30)

Compare this with Fleck, who said

> Cognition is the most socially-conditioned activity of man, and knowledge is the paramount social creation. The very structure of language presents a compelling philosophy characteristic of that community, and even a single word can represent a complex theory. . . . every epistemological theory is trivial that does not take the sociological dependence of all cognition into account in a fundamental and detailed manner. (Fleck 1935, p. 42)

Fleck went further than Durkheim in analyzing the idea of a social group. He introduced several specialized terms: the thought collective (equivalent to Durkheim's social group) and its thought style (equivalent to Durkheim's collective representations), which leads perception and trains it and produces a stock of knowledge.

For Fleck, the thought style sets the preconditions of any cognition, and it determines what can be counted as a reasonable question and a true or false answer. It provides the context and sets the limits for any judgment about objective reality. Its essential feature is to be hidden from the members of the thought collective.

> The individual within the collective is never, or hardly ever, conscious of the prevailing thought style which almost always exerts an absolutely compulsive force upon his thinking, and with which it is not possible to be at variance. (Fleck 1935, p. 41)

Fleck's thought style is very close to the idea of a conceptual scheme, which according to some philosophers limits and controls individual cognition so severely as to exclude transcultural communication. For Fleck the thought style is as sovereign for the thinker as Durkheim held collective representation to be in primitive culture, but Fleck was not talking about primitives.

For Durkheim the division of labor accounts for the big difference between modern and primitive society: to understand solidarity we should examine those elementary forms of society that do not depend on exchange of differentiated services and products. According to Durkheim, in these elementary cases individuals come to think alike by internalizing their idea of the social order and sacralizing it. The character of the sacred is to be dangerous and endangered, calling every good citizen to defend its bastions. The shared symbolic universe and the classifications of nature embody the principles of authority and coordination. In such a system problems of legitimacy are solved because individuals carry the social order around inside their heads and project it out onto nature. However, an advanced division of labor destroys this harmony between morality, society, and the physical world and replaces it with solidarity dependent on the workings of the market. Durkheim did not think that solidarity based on sacred symbolism is possible for industrial society. In modern times sacredness has been transferred to the individual. These two forms of solidarity are the basis of the main typology in Durkheim's theory (Durkheim 1893, 1895).

Fleck distinguished the thought collective, comprising the true believers, from the thought community, formally members of the first but not necessarily under the constraints of the thought style. Then he allowed for thought collectives to vary according to their persistence over time, from the most transient and accidental to the most stable formations. He considered the thought style of the stable formations to be more disciplined and uniform, as in the guilds, trade unions and churches. Fleck went to some pains to discuss the internal structure of groups; an inner elite of ranked initiates exists at the center, the masses on the outside edge. The center is the moving point. The periphery takes its ideas in an unquestioning, literal sense; ossification occurs at the rim. He envisaged many thought worlds, each with its center and rim, intersecting, separating, and merging. Somewhat parallel to moral density in Durkheim's theory, Fleck recognized that the sheer amount of interaction could vary; the degree of concentration and energy at the center depends on the pressure of demand from the outer fringes. When this interaction is strong, the question of individual deviation hardly arises. Fleck was not interested in sacredness or in social evolution. Nonetheless he applied the Durkeimian idea of a sovereign thought style to modern society, even to science. This would have horrified Durkheim. As Fleck said, the Durkheimians exhibited "an excessive respect, bordering on pious reverence, for scientific facts" (pp. 46–47). He ridiculed their attitude as a naive obstacle to the building of a scientific epistemology.

Durkheim's sayings often invoke a mysterious, superorganic group mind. Fleck cannot surely be charged with the same failing. His approach was entirely positivistic. In dealing with the criticisms that affect them both, a good strategy is to get Durkheim and Fleck to make a common defense. Sometimes Fleck has the best answer, sometimes Durkheim. Fighting as allies, back to back, each can supplement with his strength the weakness of the other.

In his preface, the editor-translator of Fleck's book compares its initial rejection by reviewers with the instant and resounding success of Karl Popper's *Logic der Forschung*, published at about the same time (Trenn 1979, p. x). The different reception could largely be explained by the relative strength of the thought collective to which each writer belonged. Popper was a well-known figure in the prestigious company of Viennese philosophers and Fleck a rank outsider to philosophy. The biographical sketch describes Fleck as "a humanist with an encyclopedic knowledge" (Fleck, pp. 149–53). A medical doctor and a bacteriologist whose publications and research were about the serology of typhus and syphilis and various pathogenic organisms, he was not well placed to impress the philosophers. It would be more Durkheimian to follow out Fleck's own idea that the thought collective, that is, the social organization, explains the lack of attention he first received. Nonetheless, it is interesting to follow the editor's idea that its initial failure was a matter of incompatible thought styles. Indeed, it seems that the original reviewers faulted Fleck for a reductionist minimization of the individual scientist's role. He was reproached for his neglect of individual personalities in the history of science. His sociological analysis was dismissed as adding little to what Max Weber had already said. All in all, he was criticized for his whole message and not for any incidental elements. The strong demand he made for sociological and comparative epistemology was dismissed. His editors believe that times have changed and that now a decisive shift in thought style has occurred.

Certainly there is a new interest in distinct styles of reasoning in the history of science. Galileo introduced a new style of thought which rendered old questions impossible. Ian Hacking's chapter "Language, Truth and Reason" (1982) briefly surveys a number of recent, influential essays in the history of science on "new modes of reasoning that have specific beginnings and trajectories of development" (p. 51). In most cases, however, the tendency is to be interested in the thought style and not in its relation to the thought collective. If the shift in Fleck's direction is going to be creative, it must not separate thought style from thought collective, thus failing again the sociological part of the enterprise.

Thomas Kuhn was the first since 1937 to draw attention to Fleck's book by a reference (Kuhn 1962). In his foreword to the English translation he voices hesitations that will still be widely shared. Fleck's position, he said, is not free of fundamental problems.

> . . . for me these cluster, as they did on first reading, around the notion of a thought collective . . . I find the notion intrinsically misleading and a source of recurrent tension in Fleck's text. Put briefly, a thought collective seems to function as an individual mind writ large because many people possess it (or are possessed by it). To explain its apparent legislative authority, Fleck therefore repeatedly resorts to terms borrowed from discourse about individuals. (Kuhn 1979, p. x)

In sum, thinking and feeling are for individual persons. However, can a social group think or feel? This is the central, repugnant paradox. Kuhn appreciates in Fleck's book a number of separate insights, but not Fleck's main argument. By rejecting it, Kuhn is sharing discomfort with many liberals. John Rawls' philosophy of justice is founded on outright individualism; in his view society is not "an organic whole with a life of its own distinct from and superior to that of all its members in their relations with one another" (Rawls 1971, p. 264).

It is true that there are now several movements of ideas in the direction to which Fleck was urgently pointing. For instance, we can deal more easily with the uncomfortable terms. The translators considered and rejected several alternatives for *denkkollectiv*, such as "school of thought" or "cognitive community," before they adopted the literal translation," thought collective." But now the term "world" has acquired the right sense. Thought world (including distinguishable theology worlds, anthropology worlds, and science worlds) in place of thought collective would be faithful to Fleck's essential idea, while linking it appropriately to Nelson Goodman's *Ways of Worldmaking* (Goodman 1978) and to Howard Becker's *Art Worlds* (Becker 1982). Fleck's subject was scientific discovery, Becker's is artistic creativity, and Goodman's is cognition in general.

Each of these very independent thinkers has a striking affinity with the others. Becker insists that collective effort produces a work of art, even though it is attributed to a particular artist. He includes in the art world, along with the artist, the anonymous collaboration of the suppliers, the canvas makers, the paint manufacturers, the framers, the distributors, the catalogue designers, the galleries, and the public. It is a historical chance that the one class of actors in the art world of Western painting should be individually named and renowned as the "artists." In other art worlds in other times and places, the collectivity of the studio or the mastercraftsmen's guild overbears the individual's fame. All art worlds depend on the existence of a public for the art work. The interaction with public demand is a crucial and creative part of the music or painting world. Fleck took the same point, emphasizing both the role of laboratory practice and of public support.

> Had it not been for the insistent clamor of public opinion for a blood test, the experiments of Wassermann would never have enjoyed the social response that was absolutely essential to the development of the reaction, to its "technical perfection," and

to the gathering of collective experience. Laboratory practice alone readily explains why alcohol and later acetone should have been tried besides water for extract preparation, and why healthy organs should have been used besides syphilitic ones. Many workers carried out these experiments almost simultaneously, but the actual authorship is due to the collective, the practice of cooperative and team work. (Fleck 1935, pp. 77–78)

He even went so far as to enjoin anonymity and self-effacement on all scientists. This democratic ideal may partly explain why he chose the Russian model of a collective farm to describe the science worlds.

Nelson Goodman argues that the rightness of categories depends on their fitting within a world. Rightness, meaning fit with action and fit with other categories, is parallel to Fleck's idea of harmony between elements within a thought style. It almost parallels Fleck's idea that truth, in a sense, is made from illusions (a phrase that troubled Kuhn). The way that Fleck explained the construction of objective reality by the social experiences of the thought collective is very close to Goodman's explanation of rightness as fit with practice:

Without the organization, the selection of relevant kinds, effected by evolving tradition, there is no rightness or wrongness of categorization, no validity or invalidity of inductive reference, no fair or unfair sampling, and no uniformity or disparity among samples. Thus justifying such tests for rightness may consist primarily in showing not that they are reliable but that they are authoritative. (Goodman 1978, pp. 138–39)

Anthropologists have used modes of thought to refer to the same authoritatively interlocked words and ideas (Horton and Finnegan 1973).

It is now easier to use science worlds, art worlds, music worlds, or thought worlds, instead of thought collective, for the social grouping that is defined by its distinctive thought style because it invokes these contemporary supporting links for Fleck's central idea.

The stage may be well set, but the Durkheim-Fleck program

in the sociology of knowledge fails if it is based on fundamental error. Two grave objections are commonly made against it. The first objection is the argument against loose functional explanations. Durkheim's central thesis, that religion maintains the solidarity of the social group, is a functional explanation. Fleck has his own version of a self-sustaining functional loop:

> The general structure of a thought collective entails that the communication of thoughts within a collective irrespective of content or logical justification, should lead for sociological reasons to the corroboration of the thought structure (Fleck 1935, p. 103)

They were both functionalists: the question rises, do their arguments fail to provide the necessary logical steps? If not, could a better functionalist argument be made that would justify their conclusions?

The second objection concerns the rational basis for collective action. If individuals are assumed to be rational and seeking their self-interest, do they ever make sacrifices on behalf of the group? And if they do act against their self-interest, what theory of human motivation would explain it? Durkheim brings in religion to do some of the explaining. For Fleck, any system of knowledge is a kind of public good, and consequently, religion itself raises the same problems. For both, the real issue is the emergence of the social order itself. The pages that follow will not concern anyone who holds that the social order springs spontaneously into being. The theory of rational choice forbids spontaneous commitment to be shipped into the argument under guise of religion. The commitment that subordinates individual interests to a larger social whole must be explained. To many readers of Durkheim, his argument seems to depend too heavily on religion. and if, for the purposes of their sociological epistemology, religious belief is to be equated with any other knowledge system, then Fleck's assertion that a thought style reigns sovereign over its thought world seems also to be suspect. How did that sovereignty arise? This is what rational choice theorists require to be explained.

On the other hand, the theory of rational choice has severe limitations. People do not seem to act according to its principles (Hardin 1982). The program of Durkheim and Fleck can answer the functionalist criticism and the rational choice criticism only by developing a double stranded view of social behavior. One strand is cognitive: the individual demand for order and coherence and control of uncertainty. The other strand is transactional: the individual utility maximizing activity described in a cost-benefit calculus. In most of this volume we will say little about the latter, which is already well represented in scholarly writing. The underrepresented case is the role of cognition in forming the social bond.

2

Smallness of Scale Discounted

SMALL-SCALE SOCIETIES are different. Many who are well apprised of the difficulty of explaining collective action within the theory of rational choice are content to make exceptions. Smallness of scale gives scope to interpersonal effects. The whole field of psychology is located here, along with irrational emotions. When the scale of relations is small enough to be personal anything can happen, and rational choice theory recognizes the limits of its domain. Consequently, there seems to be no theoretical problem about altruism when the social organization is very small. However, on close examination the exempting of small scale societies from the force of rational analysis does not stand up well to criticism. They cannot be exempted any more than can religious organizations. The objective in this chapter is to extend the rational choice arguments so as to open up the no-go areas where the theory is not supposed to run. Then the theory stands bare. It will be faced inescapably with acute difficulties that cannot be concealed by reference to scale, or to religious, emotional, or irrational factors. This step is necessary for confronting the awkward empirical record. We know that individuals do submit their private interests to the good of others, that altruistic behavior can be observed, that groups have an influence on the thinking of their members and even develop distinctive thought styles. This we know, without having a theory of behavior that takes it into account.

In what follows we will apply Mancur Olson's analysis of collective action to the issues usually disguised by scale effects. In *The Logic of Collective Action* (1965) he starts from the economic theory of public goods, but he ends with a general theory of collective action. Public goods are a hybrid concept in economic theory. The term was adapted to defining legitimate government spending. If revenue has been collected to serve public purposes, these must be distinguished from individual benefits and brought under public legislative control. A public good should benefit all, as does, for example, clean air, or it should at least be available to all, as for example, the public highway. Starting with examples chosen to illustrate the particular policy problem, the concept was founded on three complex and distinct notions: first, that the supply of the good is undiminished by individual consumption; second, that no one party can claim refund for having produced it since it is provided by the collectivity; and third, no member of the collectivity can be excluded from using it. Essentially it is a kind of good that escapes the price mechanism and so eludes standard economic analysis.

According to Olson's general formulation, an individual behaving according to rational self-interest will not contribute to the collective good more than will produce the benefit that he wants in his own interest. This is for two distinct reasons. One argument depends on the nature of public goods, the problems that arise from the need for cooperation to provide them, and the impossibility of excluding anyone from enjoying them once they are produced. The other argument depends on diminishing returns for each person who has contributed to the production as the number of persons enjoying the product increases. The first case is very strong. The second, based on effects of scale, needs to be qualified. Separating these two issues, let us begin by considering the first set of problems that arise from the nature of public goods. Olson argues that in-so-far as his contribution will not be enough to produce the collective good, and in-so-far as its production depends, by definition on many contributors, the individual's rational calculation will tend to stop him from providing any of it. For one reason, his own contribution is of small consequence. As he can expect that the absence of his own mite will make no difference, he can hope to take a free ride on the contributions of the others. "Let George do it" is the principle of Olson's inconsequentiality theorem. For another reason, he can expect the others to fall for the same temptation to take a free ride, and so, if their contributions are not forthcoming, his own will be wasted. In these cases, the low probability of collaboration has nothing to do with scale.

These arguments cogently explain a lot of the difficulties faced by voluntary organizations. Although he has analyzed them so well, Olson himself puts more weight on the argument from scale. It is true that in certain cases the benefit to each user is diminished by every increase in the total number of users. Public highways and parks are clear cases in which crowding curtails enjoyment. But this does not apply to other kinds of public goods, such as national defense, police protection, street lighting, or trade unions negotiating on behalf of workers in a particular industry. It may not apply to education if it be conceded that the benefits accruing to each educated person are multiplied by increased opportunities of educated discourse. It certainly does not apply to the creation of a social order. The more persons who can be involved in the system of trustfulness, the more advantages for each. This is the most telling issue for the question of how collective action can be explained. Olson's case stands far more strongly on the problems of trust created by the possibility of free-riding, and this applies to instances that are very small-scale indeed.

According to Olson, the problems of collective action as stated in the theory of rational choice can only be solved by coercion, or by activity that is a low-cost by-product of entrepreneurial actions directed to individual selective benefits, or by a mixture of both. A community that has neither of these stimuli is plagued by indecision and dissension. Each rational individual deciding to be a member, knowing that no sanctions can be applied against him and that there are no special rewards for public service, will be calculating whether he could do better for himself on his own. When this is the case for all members, the group must remain latent. As such, it can muster a concerted effort for a short-term activity—fundraising or protesting—but not much more.

Olson exempted religious organization from his general theory. But twenty years later the exception of religious organization is clearly a mistake. The history of religion best bears out his theory. Whenever religious organizations have had access to coercive powers or have been able to offer selective rewards of wealth or influence to their most dedicated individual members, their religions have had a stable and flourishing career. And whenever these have been absent, for whatever reason, the history is one of continual friction and schism (Douglas and Wildavsky 1982). It does not help our understanding of religion to protect it from profane scrutiny by drawing a deferential boundary around it. Religion should not be exempted at all.

Olson is also willing to exempt small groups from the implications of his theory. He gives a decisive influence to scale of organization (Chamberlin 1982), and at a certain point of diminishing scale expects his observations not to apply. If small-scale communities are to be exempted, as well as religious ones, then what Durkheim has to say would not be relevant, since he based his arguments on both.

There is further a common belief that in something called "community" individuals can disinterestedly collaborate with one another and construct a collective good. Within such a community, the dictates of rational choice do not apply. This is an extraordinarily powerful emotive idea.

These apparently minor exceptions from analytic probing represent an uncharted land in which one may wander as one pleases. Such freedom is damaging to Durkheim's and Fleck's project. The exemptions are not minor or unimportant. Acceptance of them blunts the force of the whole inquiry. In particular, they deflect attention from Olson's interesting and pessimistic concept of the latent group. No one who is interested in explaining collective action can lightly dismiss the formidable problems faced by a small community trying to stay in being. Worse, identifying the exempted areas of social life as those that are small in scale implies that in modern times they are few and trivial. But this is disingenuous. We are talking about systematic constraints on collaboration that apply on a huge gamut, from the local Parent Teachers' Association to labor unions, to parliamentary constituencies, and to international cooperation (Olson 1965, pp. 66–131). The scale of latent groups in modern society is vast; the consequences of their failure to coalesce are momentous. So we should nerve ourselves to enter the fenced-off preserve. Religion can be partly left to one side at this point, because religious organization only too obviously does not constitute any exception to the general case and because some specific things will be said about religion and sacredness in later chapters. This is the point at which to concentrate on scale effects.

The faulty argument can be expressed as follows. Smallness

of scale fosters mutual trust; mutual trust is the basis of community; most organizations, if they do not have a base in individual selective benefits, start as small, trustful communities. Then the special characteristics of community solve the problem of how the social order can ever emerge. Many maintain that after the initial birth through the community experience, the rest of social organization can be explained by complex interlocking of individual sanctions and rewards. Olson himself seems to subscribe to this view. The two big difficulties with accepting it are empirical and theoretical. In practice, small-scale societies do not exemplify the idealized vision of community. Some do, some do not foster trust. Has no one writing on this subject ever lived in a village? Ever read any novels? Tried to raise funds? To be sure, there are successful communities, but it goes counter to the spirit of rational inquiry to select only the cases that fit and to neglect the many others. One may wonder if this is a form of inquiry or an ideology or a quasi-religious doctrine. It will provide a pertinent example of a set of ideas that acquire their validity and therefore their power from recognizable uses within institutions rather than from the force of reason. For the appeal to the small, idealized, intimate community is strong in political rhetoric.

Michael Taylor has the special merit of having treated the social order as a public good. He is also among many who believe that small communities are a form of society where rational self-interest does not dictate the outcome of decisions (1982). Given only that it be small enough and stable enough, members of the community are thought freely to make contributions that they would withhold in larger and more fluid conglomerations. This formula is somewhat question-begging, because the issue is how that community gets to be stable. Taylor has analyzed three kinds of communities. There are the modern communes (or intentional communities), which many have studied. Second, there are peasant societies, which have generated a whole cottage industry of scholarship. Third, there are small-scale tribal societies described in anthropological literature. All three types have a documentation so vast, varied, and weighted with detail that most philosophers understandably shun it, and so the idea that small communities are exempt from the analysis of rational behavior tends to be unembarrassed by criticism.

Taylor starts by locating community at the small-scale end of a continuum of elements that are each vulnerable to increase of scale. So the community is by definition small, face-to-face in its interactions, and many-sided in its relationships. Second, participation in its decision-making processes is widespread. Third, the members of a community hold beliefs and values in common; its most perfect example would be fully consensual. Fourth, it holds together by virtue of a network of reciprocal exchanges.

Taylor asserts that these arrangements render rational choice analysis inapplicable.

> In many small-scale communities no "selective incentives" or controls are needed: it is rational to cooperate voluntarily in a production of the public good of the social order. (Taylor 1982, p. 94)

Beyond the blunt assertion that that the individuals who would stand to gain from the public good do actually combine to produce it, we need to know what are the steps of their negotiations with one another. Any particular social order involves contentious issues of justice and morals. Taylor supposes that these are resolved in very small communities by instituting economic equality and by wide participation in public matters.

To maintain this position about tribal society he would need to exclude government by secret associations, cliques, and cabals, which amounts to some large and arbitrary deletions from his own instances of community. He further implies that in real community, physical coercion is absent. It depends on what he counts as coercive. Unless coercion is given a very narrow meaning, it would be wise to drop most small-scale tribal societies from this definition of community. In most wandering bands of hunters, it is true, equality and participation are well exemplified. But in these hunting bands, it is not specifically smallness of scale but other factors that create the conditions favorable for a non-coercive communal life. Sparsity of population, abundance of the wherewithal to satisfy wants at a low level, plus easy movement between bands allows conflict to be diffused by separation (Service 1966; Lee and DeVore 1968). These are very like the conditions in which Olson's theory expects latent groups to abound: nothing much for an individual to gain or lose by staying with the group, easy switches of allegiance, easy resistance to attempted coercion by threatening to secede. Their low level of energy expenditure and the small degree to which their existence has made a dint in the environmental resources suggest corroboration of at least the thesis that when conditions are thus favorable to individuals, not much is achieved in the way of collaboration.

David Hume has said that the problem of collective action can best be solved in very small communities because they have few possessions to quarrel about. This also goes to score a point in support of the other argument: small communities have failed to create much visible evidence of collective benefit. When we move away from the special case of mobile bands of hunters, other small-scale communities are not conspicuously successful in creating a social order that effectively protects the few persons and their modest possessions.

In the perspective of anthropology, the favorable factors have less to do with scale and more to do with the ratio of population to resources, together with a possibility of satisfying wants without engaging anyone in the hard, monotonous, sustained kind of work that tempts some to coerce the service of others. Yet it would be quite wrong to write those communities down as latent groups in Olson's sense. They really do form persisting and effective moral communities. Something else is happening that does not defy analysis and has nothing to do with scale, but which is overlooked because of the false plausibility of scale effects.

Suppose a form of social order has somehow been realized: then at the second stage Michael Taylor lists four ways in which community works to maintain it. Many other writers would subscribe to this list. None of them makes a convincing case. The first of these allegedly extrarational forms of social control is based on threats and offers. These are no more or less than appeals to individual's self-interest. This process is indeed very well documented by anthropologists, but their analysis is much too compatible with mainline rational choice theory to justify the exempting of small communities from its force.

The second way in which the social order is frequently said to be maintained is by socialization. Adults are exposed to public shaming, and children are put through painful initiations which train them in the right attitudes. But we can wonder how the parents are ever induced to let their children undergo the standard torments and indignities. Collective sanctions are a form of collective action. Withdrawing from the process of socialization is another way of not cooperating. What happens when one mother claims that her little boy is too sensitive or too young? What stops her from withdrawing her kid and all the other mothers from withdrawing theirs in a headlong rush away from socialization? The answer is their commitment to the given social order. But is not this collective choice just what we are trying to explain?

The third way in which the social order is allegedly maintained in primitive societies is through the structural characteristics of those societies. This is a subtle point. These characteristics are not specific mechanisms of social control; they cannot be separated from what is controlled, but they provide a framework for the social controls. Essentially they are the patterns of reciprocity, kinship, and marriage. However, these exchange patterns are the articulation of the social order, which itself is only an articulation of behavior, so the argument is circular. It can only be saved by an explicit functionalist assumption of a self-maintaining system of interlocked activities.

The most widely attested feature of primitive society that is said to maintain the social order is the belief in supernatural sanctions, such as fear of witchcraft, sorcery, or punitive ancestors. If the other arguments fail, and these beliefs are left to carry the main burden of the case separating community from the rest of social behavior, the whole argument has been handed over to irrational factors. Either the creation of community is something that only primitives can do, thanks to their superstitious beliefs in witchcraft and ancestors, or such beliefs have to be generalized in a way that also applies to modern society.

The orthodox anthropological interpretation, which was accepted right through the 1960s, assumed a self-stabilizing model in which every item of belief plays its part in maintaining the social order. However, some interesting upheavals in the last quarter century have thrown doubt on the existence of tendencies making for equilibrium in the societies studied by anthropologists. One factor is the theoretical development of the subject and its dealing with new findings. Among these, the most relevant is the growth of critical Marxist anthropology whose historical materialism rejects the homeostatic emphases of the earlier generation. (Abramson 1974; Bailey and Llobera 1981; Bloch 1975; Friedman 1979; Godelier 1973; Meillassoux 1981; Sahlins 1976; Terray 1969). Another important factor is the end of colonialism. Another is the development of fieldwork in New Guinea, a country that had not been colonized prior to anthropological research. Now it is possible to stand aside and assess the effect of colonial government on all individual incentives and on the use of force.

Of course, in colonial conditions it used to be easier to imagine the non-coercive community. Subject peoples were no more allowed their former profitable trade in guns, ivory, and slaves. They were no more allowed to contend for glory in headhunting or daring cattle raids, and no more to set ambushes, steal wives, or execute violent revenges. In the colonial economy, in which the only economic incentive to work was a low income for cash cropping, it was easy to suppose that the original community had not offered individual incentives for gain. The current, more sophisticated, anthropological record shows these small-scale societies as never static, nor self-stabilizing, but being built continuously by a process of rational bargaining and negotiating. The categories of political discourse, the cognitive bases of the social order, are being negotiated. At whatever point of this process the anthropologist clicks his camera and switches on his tapes he can usually record some temporary balance of satisfactions, when each individual is momentarily constrained by others and by the environment. The individual cost-benefit analysis applies inexorably and enlighteningly to the smallest micro-exchanges, with them as well as us. Anthropologists test the credibility of one another's ethnographic reports by scrutinizing the reported balance of reciprocal exchanges. Their evidence destroys the case for extrarational principles producing a community at some unspecified point of diminishing scale. It is when making threats and offers that individuals often invoke the power of fetishes, ghosts, and witches to make good their claims. The resulting cosmology is not a separate set of social controls. In Durkheim's work the whole system of knowledge is seen to be a collective good that the community is jointly constructing. This is the process we need particularly to focus upon in subsequent chapters.

At this point the common idea of the anarchic utopian community can be dismissed as a fond illusion. The anthropological evidence from small-scale societies supports the widest extension of Mancur Olson's main thesis that individuals are easily deterred from contributing to the collective good. It does not support his contention that scale is the main factor. Any attempt to probe the foundations of social order brings to light the paradoxical foundations of thought. At this level of abstraction it is not self-referencing circularity that is wrong. By trusting to the effects of scale, the argument has been derouted. It has missed the earlier logical step that would take it to questioning how systems of knowledge come into being. There is plenty of good reason to think that rational choice theory is inadequate to explain political behavior. Something is going on in civic affairs that the theory of rational choice does not capture. According to the Durkheim-Fleck position, the mistake is to have ignored the epistemological problem. Instead of supposing that a system of knowledge springs into being naturally and easily, their approach extends skepticism about the possibility of collective action to skepticism about the possibility of shared knowledge and shared beliefs. This more embracing doubt about the foundations of community points the way to an answer.

3

How Latent Groups Survive

IF SMALLNESS OF SCALE does not account for the origin of cooperative communities, perhaps something else does. To explain without explicitly supporting the functionalist approach intrinsic to Durkheim's argument and to Fleck's, several psychological and sociological suggestions have been made. However, psychological explanations must be disallowed if they bypass the axiomatic framework in which the problem is posed. So we can sweep away any invoking of processes that encourage self-sacrifice because it satisfies a psychic need to maintain self-esteem or provides the pleasure of giving pleasure to others. Such psychic satisfactions do not work reliably enough to carry the weight of explaining. If they work sometimes and sometimes do not, the question is just pushed back into the form of asking what switches on the public-spirited emotional attitudes.

Another form of explanation makes collective action depend on the complex interlocking of multiple reciprocal exchanges, direct and indirect. According to the strong form of this explanation, the rational individual is tied into a complex set of relations in which he must act trustfully because he has no choice. In the weak form, he has some choice and if he chooses against cooperation he will wreck the whole show. Then, the answer comes, social sanctions will be applied to penalize uncooperative behavior. But applying sanctions, as we saw in the case of small-scale societies, is a form of collective action and just as much in need of explaining.

The objection to the strong form stems from the notion of someone being in a no-choice situation. To be sure, it is possible and it often happens that a person is laid under such powerful coercion that there is really no choice but to obey. In such a case there is no issue involving mutual trust and no problem about free cooperation. When there is no choice, we have gone outside the case to which rational choice theory applies. Moreover, to extend this case to a wide range of collective action only fudges the problem. It also proposes an unacceptable view of human agency. It presents humans as passive agents, acting under more or less complete constraint. The argument depends on a form of sociological determinism that credits individuals with neither initiative nor sense.

It was partly for this failing that sociological functionalism has been in low repute for the last thirty years. It had no place for the subjective experience of individuals willing and choosing. To suppose that individuals are caught in the toils of a complex machinery that they do not help to make is to suppose them to be passive objects, like sheep or robots. Worse, there is no scope in such a theory for explaining change unless it comes from outside as an irresistible coercive force. To assume such stability in social relations demands too much of our credulity.

Given the poverty of alternative explanations, it behooves us to look more carefully for a form of functionalist argument that avoids these pitfalls and yet meets the needs of the Durkheim-Fleck idea of a social group that generates its own view of the world, developing a thought style that sustains the pattern of interaction.

Jon Elster has declared provocatively that it is close to impossible to find in sociology any cases of functional analysis where the presence of all the logically required features of such an explanation is demonstrated (Elster 1983). This is not just because sociologists argue carelessly, but because he believes that functionalistic explanation is not appropriate to human behavior. His argument starts with a review of types of explanation. In the domain of physics, causal and mechanistic explanations apply. In the domain of biology, causal and functional explanations apply. Functional explanations are justified by the overarching theory of natural selection. No general theory equivalent to biological evolution applies to human behavior. For reasons which he succinctly lists, humans can do things that biological organisms cannot do: they can employ strategies of waiting, they can take one step back in order to take two steps forward, and they can make other oblique moves. The explanatory type exclusively appropriate for human behavior is intentional. According to Elster, the combination of causal plus intentional theories ought to be enough for explaining whatever must be explained in human behavior. There are causal theories entertained by humans and these can be more or less mistaken. There are also intentions of humans and decisions based on the causal theories, more or less consistent, contradictory, or mistaken. The explanatory type exclusively appropriate for humans is intentional, but since Elster allows no place for self-sustaining processes or for unintended consequences that work to maintain a situation in being, so he has no place for Durkheim's and Fleck's idea of a social group unintentionally generating thoughts that sustain its own existence.

Elster has most helpfully spelled out the conditions that a correctly argued functional analysis must meet. Though they sound abstruse at first, they greatly clarify the issues. An institutional or behavioral pattern, X, is explained by its function, Y, for a group, Z, if and only if:

1. Y is an effect of X;
2. Y is beneficial for Z;
3. Y is unintended by actions producing X;
4. Y or the causal relation between X and Y is unrecognized by actors in Z; and
5. Y maintains X by a causal feedback loop passing through Z.

This list has been compiled from Robert Merton's critical analysis of functionalism (Merton 1949) and from Arthur Stinchcombe's (1968, pp. 82–83) further suggestions. Looking back on Merton's original essay and subsequent commentaries, it is amazing to see what a lot of bad functionalist argument was going around. It is not surprising that he felt impelled to introduce some methodological caution. The wildest quotations come from anthropologists; some vivid examples come from Karl Marx; and some incautious remarks come from sociologists influenced by Talcott Parsons' structural functionalism.

In Elster's view, the main explanation for the excessive and indefensible dominance of functionalism in the social sciences is historical. It is due to the prestige of biological models used in evolutionary theory. He takes pains to point out the essential differences between biological and sociological functional explanations. However, he never distinguishes between functionalist statements with genuinely explanatory intent and those that are mere rhetorical arm waving. All the colorful examples quoted by Merton from anthropologists belong in the latter class. They were used to ornament the attack that anthropologists in the 1950s wanted to make against old-fashioned ethnology (or conjectural history, as it was pejoratively described). There is no denying that they did propound a comic model deserving the mockery of Merton and Elster. According to these anthropologists absolutely everything that happens has a function in maintaining the social system in being.

Elster's step-by-step method is excellent for reducing an argument to its essentials. One argument went like this: (1) Y (more attention to food production) is an effect of X (garden magic); (2) Y is beneficial for the community, Z, that eats the food. This attempted functionalist explanation fails because no one supposes that the magic for gardening was not intended to increase the food supply. Likewise, to show that the fishing magic is intended to act as improved technology is a straight causal explanation.

A. R. Radcliffe-Brown's favorite argument that rituals have solidarity enhancing functions could be spelled out as follows:

1. Y (lineage solidarity) is an effect of X (ancestor cults);
2. Y maintains internal peace and external defense and so is good for the worshippers (Z);
3. The producers of X do not intend thereby to maintain Y;
4. Nor do they recognize any causal link by which Y maintains X.

This attempt at a functional explanation fails. What exactly is the hidden causal loop? It depends on psychological factors (which Radcliffe-Brown called "ritual attitudes"). Performing this cult is supposed to produce the kind of emotions that contribute to solidarity. The case for ritual stimulating the emotions is weak. Hasn't anyone ever been bored in church? It is important to notice that this clearly goes against Durkheim's principles of sociological method (Durkheim 1895). Social facts must be explained by social facts. Dipping at will into the psychological level was precisely what Durkheim's method aimed to stop. Durkheim evaded his own rules of method by making the sacred depend for its vitality on the emotional excitement of great gatherings. Fleck used the more coherent principle that trust and confidence are prerequisites of communication; he thereby avoided the inconsistency of suspending rationality in order to explain the origin of rational thought in effervescent emotions stirred up by grand-scale public rituals. It is safer to follow Durkheim's teaching, rather than his practice, and safer to reject the functional explanation based on emotions that keep the system going.

Rejecting causal loops that consist of emotions would also exclude many well-entrenched branches of sociology. For example, deviance theory sometimes argues that being relegated to a socially marginal position (X) produces emotions (Y) that lead the marginalized individuals to anti-social behavior; thus the emotions create a feedback loop by which the marginalized individuals' retaliatory activity gives to the community the (unintended) benefit of clarified norms (Cohen 1980). The functional argument depends on the unconvincing loop connecting social and psychological effects. Furthermore, it is difficult to contend that clarified norms were not part of the intended result.

Close inspection of alleged social functions of ancestor worship brings the same weakness to light. Was it ever plausible to suppose that the worshippers have no intention of producing social solidarity? Of course they do. Praying at the foot of the altar, the ancestor worshippers explicitly declare the ancestors are angered by quarreling among their descendants. They are speaking to one another obliquely. Instead of a bad and incomplete argument about hidden self-sustaining mechanisms, we now recognize a good one about intentional efforts at persuasion. However, we have no reason for believing that the public statements about solidarity will promote it. If rituals do not produce the required emotions, the ritualists could be wasting their time. It seems to be very difficult for these early Durkheimian anthropologists to make a complete functional explanation. The anthropologists cited by Merton and by those who go on to cite Merton's citations were trying to justify religion by its practical effects. Alas! Religions do not always make believers more loyal to their rulers or more industrious in their gardens and boats, any more than magic always brings fishes to the nets. Sometimes it does, sometimes not. The charge of irrationality against primitive religion was in the minds of those anthropologists (Firth 1938). The only defense they could imagine for the religion of the people they studied was not that it was rationally intelligible, but that it had some solidarity-enhancing, courage-inducing, and work-stimulating side effects (Firth 1940). These anthropologists get the worst of both worlds. They fail to produce a good functionalist argument. They also founder on the criticism of rational choice theory, as follows.

The best that Radcliffe-Brown can do to justify belief in ancestors is to construct a fully intentional system (Radcliffe-Brown 1945). He says that the faithful have collaborated in order to create something they all want, and he assumes that they were successful. But this is precisely what has to be explained. The priests and worshippers are trying to do the very thing that in Olson's political theory is supposed to be impossible or very unlikely. They want to engage in collective action. They are rational individuals, the ancestor worshippers, each with his own preferences about how the others should treat him and how he wants to treat them. The question is, how do they ever manage to create that collective good—an agreement about ancestors. The same question applies to an agreed belief in taboos or fishing magic, sin or sacraments, one God or Three-in-One. How do they establish their collective church with its peculiar doctrines instead of each losing all in destructive heresy hunting? They are like the farmers who graze their sheep on common land. If each farmer grazes as many sheep as he likes, the land will be overgrazed and they will all be worse off. It is in their interests to cooperate, but they cannot rely on their fellows to exercise restraint, so each might as well take what he can, while he can. For lack of trust and lack of solidarity, such land gets overgrazed to the last blade of grass. In other contexts, manufacturers who like clean air do not voluntarily charge themselves with the costs of cleaning up their own processes. Houseowners cannot be counted on voluntarily to shovel snow off sidewalks in front of their own door step. In matters of religious doctrine, the equivalent case is for each individual to claim a private understanding with God and to reject the doctrines that conflict with his preferred beliefs. The logical and practical problem of how collective action is ever achieved applies just as much to religion as to other theories of the world. Religion does not explain. Religion has to be explained. We cannot allow Durkheim and Fleck and their friends to brush the main problem aside without more justification. Like everyone else, they must spell out the logical steps of their case or accept the charge of mysticism and appeal to the irrational.

Forcing them to make a common defense has a singular advantage. Durkheim could avoid the question of collective action because he was dealing with primitives and religion. What he said about these topics was not supposed to apply to secular beliefs in the modern world. But he is a broken reed when it comes to understanding our own collective action. He never tried to apply his theory to us. We may be tempted to suppose with Durkheim that scientific ideas force their evidence upon our experiments. We know that this runs counter to the history of science and to the tracing of distinctive thought styles. Fleck was more up-to-date in insisting that a scientific fact does not smack the researchers between the eyes and compel assent. He showed that it took four centuries before scientific advances in other fields were important enough to establish a definitive distinction between different diseases originally clumped together as venereal:

> Such entrenchment of thought proves that it was not so-called empirical observation that led to the construction and fixation of the idea. (Fleck 1935, p. 3)

A combined Durkheim-Fleck approach to epistemology prevents either science or religion from being accorded too much privilege. Both science and religion are equally joint products of a thought world; both are improbable achievements unless we can explain how individual thinkers combine to create a collective good.

One of the criticisms against Olson's case is the practical evidence that groups which, on his showing, ought to be counted as latent and therefore only ought to manifest existence sporadically, actually do survive, and do create and sustain some common cultural achievement. The bands of hunters in Australia, Borneo, the Congo or Amazon basins cannot count as latent groups. They really have made a common culture, perhaps not rich in material achievements, but not to be dismissed either. Thanks to Elster's guidance on functionalism, we can construct a true Durkheimian-style functionalist argument to explain why certain beliefs emerge to be held in common and so enable latent groups to achieve some degree of communal efficiency. The argument that follows may seem elliptical. It depends on documentation that has been fully discussed elsewhere about beliefs in witchcraft and sorcery and about sectarian beliefs in a cosmic evil conspiracy (Douglas 1963; Douglas and Wildavsky 1982; Douglas 1986).

The first difficulty that Olson's latent group encounters is that its members, by definition, have not got any strong personal interest in remaining in it. If the costs of membership increase beyond the expected benefits, the threat to withdraw is their big bargaining chip. They can use it against anyone who tries to extract from them more contributions than they want to make. Any member who particularly wants the latent group to survive will be vulnerable to others' threat to secede. Consequently the affairs of a latent group will tend to be conducted by veto and backed by threats of withdrawal. Leadership will be weak because of a tendency for the great to be exploited by the small.

The first step is to reformulate the above as a functionalist explanation of the weak leadership.

Cycle A
1. Y (weak leadership) is an effect of X (a credible threat to withdraw from Z).
2. Y is useful for Z in enabling rational individuals to resist unwelcome demands upon their private resources.
3. Y is unintended (and actually deplored).
4. Y is unrecognized as an effect of X.
5. By an unseen causal loop, Y (weak leadership) maintains X (the tendency to threaten withdrawal) because it prevents the development of coercive regulations.

This explains one difficulty (weak leadership) that such a group experiences in achieving its common goals. On the other hand, if making coercion impossible counts as an achievement, it has achieved a certain amount. Such a community at this point would do well to institute selective benefits for individuals according to Olson. They could plan to have many other common goals achieved as by-products of self-interested entrepreneurship. This may simply not be possible. Many sects, communes, and social groups whose circumstances conform to the model in Cycle A are found at the periphery of a larger, richer society or out in the wilds where entrepreneurship just cannot be well rewarded. In such a case, the individuals can make an alternative move that will have the effect of strengthening the community base—still acting only in accordance with self-regarding motives. The next cycle also reformulates Olson's account (Olson 1965, p. 41).

Cycle B
1. Y (a stable well-defined boundary around the group) is an effect of X (insisting on equality and 100 percent participation).
2. Y is beneficial for Z (consolidating membership).
3. Y is unintended as an effect of X.
4. Y is achieved by an unperceived causal loop.
5. The boundary (Y) maintains X (the equality rule) that is instituted to control free riders. That they should have achieved enough collective action to make a rule may seem question-begging. But this is only a rule that each will apply in his own self-interested wish not to be made a sucker by free riders. It has the self-policing effects of a convention, as described in the next chapter.

This 100 percent participation, to be successfully monitored, requires stiff conditions of entry, which constitute a hurdle for would-be entrants. As a result of this second cycle, whatever possibility of individual selective benefits that there may have been is severely curtailed. The two cycles, A and B, do no more than spell out in Elster's terms the account that Olson has made of the troubles that beset latent groups and the solutions that he describes. By these two cycles, a social group with a precise and distinctive form of organization has been defined, one with no coercive power and no individual selective benefits of a material kind. By Olson's theory it is only a latent group. The stumbling block for his theory is that, in common experience, social groups corresponding perfectly to this description manifest themselves quite effectively and continuously. We will now use Elster to justify Durkheim, Fleck, and the functional anthropologists; and Elster to supplement the theory of collective action by adding the cognitive element to stabilize and legitimate the social group. Thanks to the clear description of the form of the society, we can now describe the particular pattern of beliefs that would justify the first two cycles, which would presumably emerge simultaneously.

Cycle C
1. Y (shared belief in an evil conspiracy) is an effect of X
   (mutual accusations of betrayal of the founding principles of the society).
2. Y is beneficial for Z.
3. Y is unintended.
4. Y depends on a causal connection that is not perceived by
   members.
5. The hidden causal loop is as follows: Because of weak leadership, no consensus can be mustered for formulating or
   applying laws or for punishing deviants (Cycle A). The
   threat to secede can be indirectly controlled by the
   strong boundary (Cycle B), which automatically insures
   that exit will be costly. So only oblique political action is
   possible; hence, there is the tendency to check exploita-
   tive behavior by accusing incipient faction leaders of
   principled immorality. There is nothing else that they
   can be accused of, since there are no other rules. The
   activity of accusing, X, reinforces the belief, Y, in outside
   conspiracy, but Y maintains X.

Instead of using the beliefs to explain the cohesion of the
society, we have used the society to explain the beliefs, and they
certainly needed a better explanation than by reference to real
cosmic conspiracies and satanic dangers. Lewis Coser's excellent
description of sects as a form of "greedy institution" supposes that
external dangers cause the sect to engage the wholehearted commitment of its members. But dangers are always everywhere. All
societies face dangers; not all are greedy institutions, and not all
that succeed in committing their members recognize the dangers
that are there. This analysis demonstrates that the problem starts
with the wavering commitment and not with the external danger
(Coser 1974).

Now the corporate group starts to be plausible as an actor in
its own right. It has become like the cardsharper forcing players to
pick a card against their will. This particular type of social group
thinks along certain grooves; it has a mind of its own. In choosing
to join this idealistic band of brothers, no one opts for the whole
package of behavior and beliefs. But they go together. All three
cycles are combined as follows:

1. Y (C, the belief in conspiracy) is an effect of X (A, weak
   leadership, and B, strong boundary).

2. Y is beneficial in keeping the community, Z, in being.
3. Y is unintended by Z so no insulting charge of duplicity stands against the believers.
4. The causal links are not perceived.
5. Y maintains X by actually splitting the community or expelling when treachery is suspected, producing a history to make every would-be leader nervous.

The anti-functionalist critique has been useful because it answers objections to the Durkheim-Fleck program from the theory of collective choice. The members of the latent group did not intend to construct the thought style that sustains the form of organization: it is a collective product. For its part, the theory of collective choice has been helpful for rehabilitating functionalism. The causal loop runs right through the organization, clearly restricting the actions of its members. The only initial assumption necessary was the minimal one that they would like to see the community survive without giving up their individual autonomy. The constraints in the situation only afford certain solutions. By adopting the easiest strategy, they start to move together along a path that ends in their joint construction of a thought style. Admittedly, it includes unpleasant elements—belief in a malign and unjust cosmos with evil humans in their midst. But one cannot always expect to like the results when starting to explain the origin of the social order. Furthermore, arguing on these lines invites no complaint against cynical reductionism: duplicity is not an issue. Reversing Olson's consequentiality argument, the jointness in the construction of the thought style disguises from each member of the thought world the consequentiality of his own small action. Each will be accusing his neighbor of treachery without suspecting that a commonly shared belief pattern is thereby strengthened.

A final word may be necessary to explain why the latent group and its thought style have been the focus of this chapter. It is because latency concentrates most clearly the problems of collective action within the assumptions of rational choice. On the one hand, a fully coerced social system, such as a prison, would raise no problems of collective choice. On the other hand, a system run on private, profit-seeking principles is easily understood, because such collective good as may emerge can be attributed to the by-products of individual entrepreneurial activity. In neither case is there a group built up collectively and maintained by the intentional sacrifice of individual members. It is the latter which raises the most acute problems about collective action. The latent group is the simplest form and therefore convenient to use to illustrate the work of the thought style in maintaining the system. However, it would not be true to say that the market depends entirely on individual self-regarding motives. There is the normative commitment to the market system itself, the needful fiduciary element sustaining prices and credit. Some equivalent analysis of thought style is needed to explain why forms of cheating do not destroy the market processes. Again, in a complex hierarchy, a combination of coercion, multiple cross-ties, conventions, and self-interest explain a lot, but not everything about the commitment of individuals to the larger group.

In most forms of society hidden sequences catch individuals in unforeseen traps and hurl them down paths they never chose. Examples pile up. It is quite remarkable that Elster could find so few. Apart from one freak case from economics that meets his five criteria, and one from political science, he sees the social landscape littered only with incomplete functional arguments. Even in anthropology, where the most outrageous bad arguments are found at the arm-waving stage, a solid set of empirical studies exemplify good functionalist explanation. Even in Robert Merton's book, where Elster first found the main lines of his case, there are well-finished functionalist explanations. For example, Merton describes a community that holds the purse strings of educational funds and believes in the mental inferiority of blacks. Their belief justifies them in withholding schooling from black families, and they are naively delighted when the scholarships won by their own children confirm their belief, justify their allocations, and maintain their control.

Sociology can so little afford to do without functionalist arguments that one starts to look suspiciously at the anti-functionalist platform. Why, for instance, do the wild sayings of the leading anthropologists figure so prominently in Merton's texts? By 1949 Malinowski's pretensions had already been severely cut down to size from within the ranks by Max Gluckman's diatribe against him (Gluckman 1947). Why did the already discredited sayings of Bronislaw Malinowski and A. R. Radcliffe-Brown still rate a detailed examination? Elster's use of anthropology suggests an answer; anthropology is quaint and entertaining. Merton originally cited the Hopi rain rite as a case of a ritual that performs the latent social function of rousing emotions that support solidarity. The dance does not produce rain for the parched desert, but it serves a latent social function. Following the same argument with the same illustration, Elster attributes the Hopi Rain Dance to the Trobrianders, living in fertile, well-watered islands. We suspect that if he had attributed the Trobrianders' ocean-fishing magic to the landlocked Hopi, it would not have mattered. The anthropology does not matter. It is not even interesting enough to be read. In this debate, it serves only as a stalking horse for more serious quarry, whatever that may be. Perhaps I am biased. Perhaps anthropology is a latent group that survives by belief in outside conspiracy. One thing is sure, for sociology to accept that no functionalist arguments work is like cutting off one's nose to spite one's face. Without a functionalist form of argument, we cannot begin to explain how a thought world constructs the thought style that controls its experience.

It is noteworthy that the details that passionately interest anthropologists are tedious to philosophers of science. To me as an anthropologist, the details of tribal organization do not seem intrinsically more tedious than those of the history of medicine. Anthropologists' stock accounts of adultery and incest are not more indecorous than the details of venereal disease, nor are they more physically intimate or repelling. The names of foreign peoples are no more difficult to spell and pronouce than gonorrhea, syphilis, soft chancre, and lymphogranuloma inguinale. Philosophers of science go to great trouble to learn the terminology and theories of relativity and quantum physics. Yet they pay scant attention to the social group that is the carrier of a thought style.

By classing discoveries in physics or biology as the main object of their research, philosophers of science have already adopted an implicit theory of knowledge. It is even one that has been tried and rejected elsewhere, the idea of a passive perceiver. Implicitly, they have relegated to the background the idea of the actively organizing mind, which is generally thought more useful in studying perception. So they have made things hard for themselves. From that chosen starting point, they will not be able to rise out of mass of detail that plagues them as much as it does the anthropologists. Both inquiries are too deeply sunk into low levels of abstraction to be able to handle the Durkheim-Fleck questions.

4

Institutions Are Founded on Analogy

How a system of knowledge gets off the ground is the same as the problem of how any collective good is created. In Durkheim's view the collective foundation of knowledge is the question that has to be dealt with first. According to his theory, the elementary social bond is only formed when individuals entrench in their minds a model of the social order. He and Ludwik Fleck invited trouble when they wrote of society behaving as if it were a mind writ large. It is more in the spirit of Durkheim to reverse the direction and to think of the individual mind furnished as society writ small. The entrenching of an idea is a social process. This is compatible with the prevailing notion in the philosophy of science that a theory is entrenched by its coherence with other theories. But the burden of the argument is that the whole process of entrenching a theory is as much social as it is cognitive. Conversely, the entrenching of an institution is essentially an intellectual process as much as an economic and political one. A focus on the most elementary forms of society brings to light the source of legitimacy that will never appear in the balancing of individual interests. To acquire legitimacy, every kind of institution needs a formula that founds its rightness in reason and in nature. Half of our task is to demonstrate this cognitive process at the foundation of the social order. The other half of our task is to demonstrate that the individual's most elementary cognitive process depends on social institutions.

45

Minimally, an institution is only a convention. David Lewis' definition is helpful: a convention arises when all parties have a common interest in there being a rule to insure coordination, none has a conflicting interest, and none will deviate lest the desired coordination is lost (Lewis 1968). Thus, by definition, a convention is to that extent self-policing. Whether village A holds its market on Friday or Saturday is indifferent so long as it does not hold it on the same day as neighboring village B. No one minds which side of the road is the rule for drivers, but they want there to be a rule. The idea that institutions have a self-policing start is more convincing than the idea that all problems are dispelled when the scale is small enough. But Thomas Schelling, who has done so much to draw attention to coordination (1960), has also assembled many examples to show how easily conventions that rest on a self-polic-ing foundation can be disturbed (1978). We want conventions about pedestrian crossings to exist, but we will violate them ourselves if we can do so with impunity. Enough impatient pedestrians to create a critical mass will march across and hold up the cars in defiance of traffic lights. The conditions for stable conventions to arise are much more stringent than it might seem. Communities do not grow up into little institutions and these do not grow into big ones by any continuous process. For a convention to turn into a legitimate social institution it needs a parallel cognitive con-vention to sustain it.

Institutional economics say practically nothing about legit-imation, although authority is sometimes discussed (Arrow 1974). To make the Durkheim-Fleck ideas about legitimacy available to this important new discussion, a switch in terminology is advisa-ble. Durkheim and Fleck both wrote of the social group. The term applied to any level of group organization. In the rest of this volume, institution will be used in the sense of legitimized social grouping. The institution in question may be a family, a game, or a ceremony. The legitimating authority may be personal, such as a father, doctor, judge, referee, or maître d'hôtel. Or it may be dif-fused, for example, based by common assent on some general founding principle. What is excluded from the idea of institution in these pages is any purely instrumental or provisional practical arrangement that is recognized as such. Here, it is assumed that most established institutions, if challenged, are able to rest their claims to legitimacy on their fit with the nature of the universe. A convention is institutionalized when, in reply to the question,

"Why do you do it like this?" although the first answer may be framed in terms of mutual convenience, in response to further questioning the final answer refers to the way the planets are fixed in the sky or the way that plants or humans or animals naturally behave.

It is at this time fashionable to say that social institutions encode information. They are credited with making routine decisions, solving routine problems, and doing a lot of regular thinking on behalf of individuals. This recent work is very pertinent. However, we find that there are many ways of talking about institutions as organizers of information. Sometimes it is a resource to be bought and sold. This is the approach taken by institutional economics. O. E. Williamson (1975) gave a new start to the subject with his theory of the effects of the supply of information on the organization of the market. On this theory, two factors count. One is how difficult or costly it is to obtain needful information about the market. The other is the numbers of firms. If the firms are many and information is freely available, then it pays off to be an independent contractor. If the converse holds, with only a few firms and information costly, then the costs of transaction become too high and it pays to take employment with a big firm that can reduce transaction costs and control information. In this way the individual's choice between working for profit as a self-employed contractor or working for a wage within a hierarchy is made on rational grounds after scanning the economic environment and particularly the costs of information. The analysis was inspired by H. A. Simon's famous complaint against the theory of rational choice—that it attributes to the rational agent grotesquely unrealistic capacities for handling information (Simon 1955). Human rationality is inherently bounded. Institutional organization is now widely treated as a way of solving problems arising from bounded rationality. Using Oliver Williamson's analysis as a point of departure, Andrew Schotter (1981) has rewritten the description of institutions in information theoretic terms. In this sense, information is not a more or less available commodity; it is whatever is newsworthy. The more that an item of behavior is predictable, the less information it carries. The focus of study has shifted from the flow of information (which is rather like a flow of commodities, in Williamson's sense) to studying the amount of information carried by a particular item seen against the background of standard expectations. This analysis, based on E. E. Shannon's model of

information, treats institutional structures as forms of informa-
tional complexity. Past experience is encapsulated in an institution's rules so that it acts as a guide to what to expect from the
future. The more fully the institutions encode expectations, the
more they put uncertainty under control, with the further effect
that behavior tends to conform to the institutional matrix: if this
degree of coordination is achieved, disorder and confusion disappear. Schotter presents institutions as entropy-minimizing devices.
They start with rules of thumb and norms; eventually they can end
by storing all the useful information. When everything is institutionalized, no history or other storage devices are necessary: "The
institution tells all" (Schotter 1981, p. 139).

    This is fine and highly congenial to a Durkheimian analysis.
The one snag is that it does not say how institutions ever start and
get enough stability to do all of that. Schotter thinks that they
develop quite easily from conventions and from other strategies
described in game theory. He supposes they develop naturally out
of an equilibrium of conflicting powers and interests. Schotter is
one among many others who subscribe to this contemporary version of functionalism that assumes in social forces a drive towards
equilibrium. However, the anthropologists went through this question in the 1950s and must feel dubious about presupposing any
drive for equilibrium. If there is such a drive, its realization is very
precarious. Equilibrium cannot be assumed; it must be demonstrated and with a different demonstration for each type of society.
Schotter reminds us that disorder is more probable than order.
Before it can perform its entropy-reducing work, the incipient
institution needs some stabilizing principle to stop its premature
demise. That stabilizing principle is the naturalization of social
classifications. There needs to be an analogy by which the formal
structure of a crucial set of social relations is found in the physical
world, or in the supernatural world, or in eternity, anywhere, so
long as it is not seen as a socially contrived arrangement. When the
analogy is applied back and forth from one set social relations to
another and from these back to nature, its recurring formal structure becomes easily recognized and endowed with self-validating
truth.

    Conventions may arise about the division of labor, but they
are likely to be challenged all the time unless their justifying
principle can be grounded in something other than conventions.
For example, everyone may be committed to the idea that there

should be a fixed division of labor that does not have to be renegotiated every time there is work to be done. All are likely to have
strong preferences for not doing the monotonous, high-frequency,
low prestige work (Douglas and Isherwood 1979). The natural distinction of sex specializes women for childbearing and rearing.
Pressures of efficiency and the distribution of power may well
override individual preferences so as to produce a sexual division
of labor, but whenever the coercion relaxes, the principle will be
challenged. Analogy with the complementarity of the right and left
hand and the complementarity of gender provide a great rhetorical
resource (Needham 1973). So the equation "female is to male as left
is to right," reinforces the social principle with a physical analogy.
Though the division of labor in itself is not going to take us far into
the organizing of society, this one analogy is a basic building block.
For example, the following:

female	male
left	right
people	king

From simple complementarity a political hierarchy has been derived. Further metaphoric elaborations of left and right
distinguish the northern and southern divisions of the kingdom;
they can organize the seating arrangements of the council to the
right and left of the king. Now the chief territorial divisions and
political functions have been justified upon extensions of the same
analogy (Gluckman 1941). Furthermore, the use of the same principle over and over is mutually reinforcing for each context. Ultimately, the whole system is grounded on nature, on the
preeminence of the right hand over the left, of the east over the
west, of the north over the south, and so on. The institutions lock
into the structure of an analogy from the body. The more primitive
the division of labor, the more the same analogy can be deployed
from one social context to another. In modern industrial society
the analogical relation of head to hand was frequently used to
justify the class structure, the inequalities of the educational system, and the division of labor between manual and intellectual
worker. The shared analogy is a device for legitimizing a set of
fragile institutions (Shapin and Barnes 1976).

To learn how this happens we have to watch private conflicts being resolved in a public forum. Then we see how each contestant musters public opinion to justify his or her actions against the other, and we observe the onlookers, who have no special interest in the case, listening to hear a general principle in which they can sympathize. The favorite analogy generalizes everyone's preferred convention.

In the last chapter, religious beliefs appeared as a not necessarily effective expression of individuals' wishes that there should be solidarity. No reasons of a functional kind showed that the cult of ancestors could produce solidarity. It seemed that the time and resources spent on sacrificial rites were wasted. This time a different kind of argument is ready. Ancestors operating from the other side of life provide the naturalizing analogy that seals the social conventions. The focus should be not on how they symbolize the structure of society, but on how they intervene in it. One could say that sitting back and receiving worship is usually the least time-consuming part of an ancestor's duties. The full job description includes continual, active monitoring of daily affairs in response to public demand.

Fleck insisted that the identification of syphilis was held back at one stage and at another stage forced on by public concern. Eventually, the demand for a cure for syphilis was more insistent than the demand for a cure for tuberculosis, although the latter actually killed more victims. Fleck insisted that the development of knowledge depends on how the knowledge is expected to intervene in practical life. Thinking has more to do with intervening than with representing (Hacking 1983). The same applies to ancestors: they are known by their interventions. To recognize how the institution of ancestors is a mechanism for regular intervention in social life, anyone can refer to libraries full of good ethnographies. Many of the philosopher's problems about the social origins of religious belief come from treating religion as something that goes on in church. The parallel mistake would be to isolate the ancestor cult from the whole social complex. It is true that, when it is in good working order, the configuration of ancestors projects the social structure. To say that it is a good metaphor of society does not explain why some metaphors work catalytically to promote collective action, and others do not. The metaphor is only a picture and we are not committed to a purely representing theory of knowledge. The ancestral model only becomes effective when the articulation of ancestors' actions articulates the social process.

When ancestors intervene they are usually part of a system that confirms local inheritance laws. Anyone wanting to validate his own claims has to trace his descent; anyone interested in contesting the claim has to question the genealogy. The ancestors are apparent where the action is hottest, controlling fraud and vice like armed police or vigilantes organized by each corporate lineage group. They are guardians of property rights first and of general morality second, much like the Internal Revenue Service. Their activity is known by the toll of pain which they exact for default. But, of course, the Internal Revenue Service is staffed by real live people, while the ancestors are dead by definition. The living are attributing action to them. We found the first attempt at functional analysis of ancestors wanting. Now we have come to a Marxist type of position: the ancestors are a socially necessary invention. The cult looks very like an epiphenomenon of certain relations of production. Does this improve our explanation of how the beliefs come to be accepted?

Hardly, because by adopting a Marxist position, we have now made piety a mere by-product of property claims. We have described worshippers who prefer to live in society in which rank and property are inherited; each collusively supports his claims by invoking a powerful ancestor. They collude to invent immortal beings who will punish backsliders. Using this approach their religion is a con and, by extension, this argument insults all believers. The new reef we have struck is the old objection to cynicism in reductionist explanations of religious belief.

Looking closer, even this cynical formula does not work out. When everyone has an ancestor backing him, all ancestors are devalued. Their respective strengths cancel out. Why should anyone take any notice of them?

As an alternative, the conventionalist explanation goes a long way. It would start with points of equilibrium at which everyone wants to see some sort of classification of kinsmen. One could start by supposing a minimal common need for each member of the society to have some area of autonomy respected by other descendants of a great grandfather. Let us say each wishes to be protected from the interference of uncles and aunts, cousins and brothers. By an emerging cognitive convention each will be granted credibility when he invokes his dead father to protect his personal space, so long as he respects the same claim from his brothers. Most ancestral cults only cover very minimal conventions: they do not need coercive sanctions to protect them. It is enough for their self-policing to know that the point where the ancestors' sway is denied is the point at which fighting that they would rather avoid is apt to break out. But why involve the dead? The pragmatic case is strong in itself. Why not just avoid violence, lest fighting break out? The answer is that the social convention is too transparent. It needs a naturalizing principle to confer the spark of legitimacy on what they want to do. The analogy from nature goes as follows: as natural progenitor (say wolf for lion) is to natural offspring (cubs, whelps), so live father is to live son and dead father to dead son. Extending backwards, it can justify the same relation invoked between dead father's father's father with dead father's father and dead father, according to the scale of the living persons ready to be involved in the legitimated social arrangements.

Thus the institutions survive the stage of being fragile conventions: they are founded in nature and therefore, in reason. Being naturalized, they are part of the order of the universe and so are ready to stand as the grounds of argument. Two examples have been given of these naturalized principles of social organization. One is the foundation of a primitive state on the analogy between the relation of female and male with the relation of left and right. Another is the foundation of a lineage on the analogy of the relation of genitor to offspring. Many more such analogies that confer natural status on social relations abound in anthropological literature.

In the history of logic it is commonly taught, following Mill, that the idea of resemblance has two aspects. One is based on mathematical resemblance of relations, as for example, $2:4::3:6$. The numbers are different, but the analogy holds because the formal relations are the same. Contrasted with this, there is the vaguer use of the word resemblance, which is open to all kinds of arbitrary interpretation. It is also taught that resemblance by itself is only a shaky basis for inference; surface resemblances are misleading. For example, the class of edible items includes many that look toxic and vice versa; the tomato, now indispensable in Western diet, was earlier classed with other bright red poisonous berries. Superficial resemblance is an unreliable basis for inference about the world. But the resemblances that provide favorable social analogies are primarily constituted for legitimizing social institutions, and they are not intended for inference about physical things. Moreover, the effort to build strength for fragile social institutions by grounding them in nature is defeated as soon as it is recognized as such. That is why founding analogies have to be hidden and why the hold of the thought style upon the thought world has to be secret. But let us be disabused of the idea that these analogies are based on haphazard resemblances. Their formal mathematical properties are the basis for the rich variety of constructions put on them. De Soto has shown (1960) in a series of psychological experiments that individuals are very well able to recognize in their social situations mathematical properties of similarity, complementarity, transitivity, exclusion, and inclusion. By using formal analogies that entrench an abstract structure of social conventions in an abstract structure imposed upon nature, institutions grow past the initial difficulties of collective action.

We should now consider how analogies from nature are found and, above all, how they are agreed upon. This points back to the logically prior question of how individuals ever agree that any two things are similar or dissimilar. Where does sameness reside? The answer has to be that sameness is conferred on the mixed bundle of items that count as members of a category; their sameness is conferred and fixed by institutions.

5

Institutions Confer Identity

☞ IT IS WELL SAID that individuals suffer from the bounding of their rationality, and it is true that by making organizations they extend the limits of their capacity for handling information. We have shown how institutions need to be established by a cognitive device. Mutual convenience in multiple transactions does not create enough certainty about the other person's strategies. It does not justify the necessary trust. The cognitive device grounds the institution at once in nature and in reason by discovering that the institutions' formal structure corresponds to formal structures in non-human realms.

First, for discourse to be possible at all, the basic categories have to be agreed on. Nothing else but institutions can define sameness. Similarity is an institution. Elements get assigned to sets where institutions find their own analogies in nature. On the one hand, the emotional energy for creating a set of analogies comes from social concerns. On the other hand, there is a tension between the incentives for individual minds to spend their time and energy on difficult problems and the temptation to sit back and let founding analogies of the surrounding society take over. This is something like Williamson's account of transaction costs except that in this case all the advantages lie with joining the corporate effort to make founding analogies to the work, and very little advantage lies with the privateer working under his own flag. However much they try to insulate their work, scientists are never completely free of their own contemporary society's pressures, which are necessary for creative effort. Scientific theory is the result of a struggle between the classifications being developed for professional purposes by a group of scientists and the classifications being operated in a wider social environment. Both are emotionally charged. Both kinds of classification depend on social interaction. One (that of the scientists) makes a determined effort to specialize and refine its concepts so as to make them fit for use in a discourse that differs from though it is contained within the entrenched ideas of the larger, encompassing social group. Is not this exactly what Fleck was describing in his history of the emergence of a scientific idea from mystic, moral, and social entrenchment? As we shall see in the next chapter, the scientific formulae that emerge always carry the marks of their social origins.

In the work of trying to understand, disorder and incoherence are more probable. Whenever a high degree of logic and complexity is found, it is a matter for surprise and needs to be explained. Complexity does not mean the repetitious isomorphism that recreates the same basic metaphor in all contexts. A truly complex ordering is the result of sustained effort. Some inducement must exist to explain why the effort is made. Fleck believed that the supply of intellectual work in science followed from demand, not just in respect of the quantity of work applied but in the selection of problems for research (Fleck 1935, p. 78). Let us assume that, in the absence of heavy demand (meaning, in the absence of inducements for specialized concentration), classification will meet minimum needs by taking the path of least effort. That path will quickly lead to a loose collection of social analogies drawn upon nature, and there it will peacefully come to rest.

According to Geoffrey Lloyd, this describes the state of early Greek science and medicine. Many would hold that it is only fair to Greek science to admit that social analogies drawn from nature have formed the basis of most medicine around the world until the last hundred years or so. The characteristics of early Greek speculative thought as Lloyd describes it are based on two schemata. One was a "recurrent appeal to pairs of opposites of various sorts both in general cosmological doctrine and in accounts of natural phenomena" (Lloyd 1966, p. 7). The macrocosm of the world was constructed from the contrasts of air and earth, fire and water, heat and cold. The other was by analogy, loosely understood. Lloyd says that there was little effort to distinguish between similarity and identity, or degrees of difference between modes of opposites that form exclusive and exhaustive alternatives and those that do not. The anthropologists on this subject have showed that the macrocosm of the world is constructed upon the model of society. It would have required a great effort to put the intrusive social analogies in their place. Recognition of different degrees of similarity and difference is a very specialized exercise in logic, quite separate from using logic to make the social order manifest.

Lloyd points out correctly that many primitive societies use dichotomous classifications of reality which mirror their dualist organization. Our discussion of convention above argued that even self-enforcing conventions, which everyone would like to see maintained, have little chance of survival unless they can be grounded in reason and nature. At one point near the top of any organization the structure is based ultimately on balanced opposition, as at the summit of national or international systems. But if there are no coordinating institutions or other more complex orderings, stalemate of hostile forces will be the most significant collective achievement at that level. The widespread distribution around the world of hunting peoples organized by moieties and other dual systems attests to the efforts to produce some collective good, although the attempts are not very effective. A totemic system naturalizes the principle of balance but not the idea of hierarchical relations governing the different totem clans (Lévi-Strauss 1963). For lack of incentives or opportunity to do more, people organized on a moiety basis have settled for balancing out their potential conflict. In a difficult environment this may be reckoned a notable achievement, but, in absolute terms, it is only a small organizational triumph.

Now the first argument has been pushed as far as it can go. Individual intentions to build an institution may be very good: individuals may shore up their own resolve and try to control each others' free riding by appeals to analogies based on nature. At this stage the argument dangles in the air. The same fissiparous tendencies are destructive of the common good at the intellectual level as at the level of social collaboration. How does one constructed analogy win over another? How does a system of knowledge get into orbit? How does one good idea compete with another? This is a central issue in the history of science. To have transferred the problems of the collective good to the intellectual sphere does not solve them, although it is necessary to make the transfer. The problems about sheep crowding the pastures and cars crowding the highways should be fairly restated as problems about ideas crowding upon one another, always competing and so destroying the necessary basis for inquiry.

To make a fresh start from the side of cognition, consider how the most elementary logical idea itself depends on social interaction. This is the idea of similarity or resemblance. When several things are recognized as members of the same class, what constitutes their sameness? It certainly seems circular to claim that similarity explains how things get classed together. It is naive to treat the quality of sameness, which characterizes members of a class, as if it were a quality inherent in things or as a power of recognition inherent in the mind. Anthropologists have a professional interest in the principles of folk classification. These lead into many taxonomic levels and ultimately to judgments of a moral and political nature. A foreign culture may work without having a good scientific classification. The senses in which it may be said to work are political, economic, social, ecological. For the intermeshing of practical purposes, folk classification makes a world that is reliably intelligible and predictable enough to live in. The objectives of folk classification are quite different from those of scientific classification; the latter is developed to express specialized theory generated in specialized institutions, which also have their own foundational ideas and are also grounded in nature. Each group of scientists is able to resist the temptation to rest upon the founding analogies of the outside society only to the extent that it is insulated from it. The arcane complexities of economic theory are examples of conceptual schemes that can only thrive with a large amount of acamedic insulation, even though they purport to deal with problems of the larger society. Even so, and paradoxically, the economists find themselves willy nilly producing highly specialized technical proofs of opinions that do not come from economic theory at all. For example, Francis Edgeworth was inspired to make his breakthrough in mathematical economics in the 1880s because of his conviction that utility theory was dangerously egalitarian in its current interpretation (Mackenzie 1980).

Comparison of cultures makes it clear that no superficial sameness of properties explains how items get assigned to classes. Everything depends on which properties are selected. So the unlikely threesome, the camel, the hare, and rock badger, get classed together in Leviticus 11 as animals that chew the cud, and so they would seem to belong to the class of cud-chewing ungulates; but since their hooves do not part like the rest of the class, they are excluded from it. In the same chapter, the pig is put in a class of one member; it is the only creature whose hoof does part that does not chew the cud. But this archaic religious classification and many other contemporary ones known to anthropologists owe their divisions much more to their capacity to model the interactions of the members of society than to a disinterested curiosity about the workings of nature. There is a fundamental shift to a scientific classification from a socially inspired one. The striving for objectivity is precisely an attempt not to allow socially inspired classifications to overwhelm the inquiry. There can be no smooth transition from the socially inspired to the scientific classification. The first cannot develop into the second by pressing deeper and deeper beneath the surface of things in the quest for knowledge, because the quest for knowledge is not one of its objectives (Lévi-Strauss 1962).

Anthropologists are well disposed to follow Quine's teaching that identity or sameness is conferred on objects by their being held in the embrace of a theoretical structure, but, as David Bloor says, mathematical theories are institutions, and vice versa. We would add that institutions perform the same task as theory. They also confer sameness. Once a theoretical scheme has been developed, elements that in the pre-theoretical stage were of dubious standing lose their ambiguity. They acquire definition when their regular functioning within the system is demonstrated. Quine's cogent attack on the independent status of similarity goes back to 1961 or further. Sameness is not a quality that can be recognized in things themselves; it is conferred upon elements within a coherent scheme.

Nelson Goodman in his strictures on the uses of similarity says that it is "a pretender, an imposter, a quack. It has indeed its place and its uses, but is more often found where it does not belong, professing powers it does not possess" (1972, p. 437). Medin and Murphy (1985) provide a valuable review of the psychological work on conceptual coherence, particularly useful since it seems to them to be necessary to tell fellow psychologists that sameness is not a quality which can be recognized in things themselves—it is conferred upon elements within a coherent scheme. The idea of a quality of similarity keeps resurfacing because sets of similar things are so well-established within a particular culture that their sameness has the authority of self-evidence.

Constructing sameness is an essential intellectual activity that goes unobserved. Quine gives a pleasing natural history speculation about the growth of scientific classification. He supposes that it starts from innate standards of similarity and moves by unguided trial and error to better theories and classifications. The innate similarity notion, shared by us with animals, recognizes grades of difference between sensory qualities, for example, a capacity to recognize gradations of color or spacing. Quine treats the move from such innate similarity notions to theorizing with new groupings of things into kinds as a smooth development.

Somewhere the argument is flawed. How can the ability to discriminate between shades of yellow, or to make other judgments of nearness or distance, or of other quality differences, ever lead to putting items into classes? To recognize a class of things is to polarize and to exclude. It involves drawing boundaries, a very different activity from grading. To move from recognizing degrees of difference to creating a similarity class is a big jump. The one activity can never of itself lead toward the other, any more than institutions can evolve toward a complete organizing of information by beginning from spontaneous self-policing conventions.

Quine imagines a primitive similarity standard, for example, that has the notion of fish, developed into a modified similarity standard with a class for fish that excludes whales and porpoises. As another example, he proposes a modified similarity standard that goes beyond superficial aspects by grouping marsupial mice with kangaroos and excluding ordinary mice. But whence do the primitive classes of mice and fish arise? He suggests a ripening process.

> One's sense of similarity or one's system of kinds develops and changes and even turns multiple as one matures, making perhaps for increasingly dependable prediction. And at length standards of similarity set in which are geared to theoretical science. . . . Things are similar in the later or theoretical sense to the degree that they are interchangeable parts of the cosmic machine revealed by science. (Quine 1969, p. 143).

He then goes on to discuss the experience of matching the similarity judgments to objective relations in the world. And further he considers the extent to which different branches of science need different similarity measures. He touches on the idea that the branches of science could be actually classified by the relative similarity notion proper to each and by the extent to which their different systematizations of nature are compatible and capable of meshing (p. 136). And, finally, he notes as a final stage for

> the maturity of a branch of science that it no longer needs an irreducible notion of similarity and kind. It is that final stage when the animal vestige is wholly absorbed into the theory. (p. 138)

This natural history of the growth and decline of similarity ideas would only explain a continuous version of the world. One or another perceptual quality might suddenly switch on or off while others fade gently, never all at once. In the continuous stream of sensation, discreet objects will not necessarily emerge. He has left unexplained the whole notion of logical meaning, starting with a state being itself and not another state. The deceptively smooth transition to a scientific classification is parallel to Schotter's deceptively smooth transition from conventions to stable institutions. In his *Treatise on Logic and Scientific Method* (1874) W. S. Jevons said, "The youngest child knows the difference between a hot and a cold body" (Jevons 1874, p. 24). By saying this, he has deftly slipped the idea of body into the innate quality grading of thermal properties. Quine is too clever to do that. He knows that the idea of a body or object needs more explaining. It always seems surprising that contemporary discussions of the idea of natural kinds should choose for examples of elementary perceptions isolated objects, such as an apple, or a body, an object, or an animal. The notion that it is less complicated to recognize objects than abstract relations goes back a long way. The line quoted from Jevons above goes on to say, "The dog can recognize his master. . . . The dignity of intellect begins with separating points of agreement from those of difference. . . . Logical abstraction, in short, comes into play and the mind becomes capable of reasoning. . . . At the same time arise general notions of classes of objects." Given the persuasiveness of Quine's principle—that kinds are parts of working theory and not independent elements—we would not expect objects to emerge at all before some theory of the world starts to classify them. And it would be more consistent with Quine's teaching not to focus the question of natural kinds on items that have already been sorted into kinds by our own culture. The problem of natural kinds surely begins with the elementary classification processes and the principles used for sorting. A theory of the world would need to start with dividing, not with grading.

In Melanie Klein's account of an infant's first attempts to find order in the world, the dominant preoccupation is not to ascertain quality spacings (Klein 1975). It may be important to begin to ask, "Is this state warmer than that? Is that state colder than this?" But the baby from the start is confronted with the problem of inductive rightness. It needs to pick out of the crowd of present sensations some practical basis for projecting forward (to use Nelson Goodman's term), a version of the world that works (Goodman 1983). The baby has no habits to rely on, and there is no existing version to be remade.

Matching samples will not lead to discriminating kinds. According to Klein, the urgent thing is to know which painful and pleasant experiences come from inside and which from outside. The first basis of projectible kinds is the difference between self and not-self (Klein, 1975). Is this warm, full sense of food a sensation that I have produced on my own? Or have I actually incorporated something that was external? Will the next confrontation end, as sometimes before, with successful incorporation and sleep? Or will it be a stormy scene ending, as sometimes before, in gripe and rage?

John Stuart Mill quotes Coleridge's account of how he analyzed contemporary politics for the *Morning Post*, using the comparison of agreement and differences; he classed France under Napoleon with Rome under the first Caesars, the Spanish Revolution with the war of the United Provinces with Philip II, and so on. Mill did not think the system of agreement and difference to be a sound method of arriving at military, prediction because of the unsystematic choice of analogies (Mill 1888). For the infant, such classifying is the only method for gradually differentiating the other and the self. The questions it asks resemble military intelligence. It needs to know whether the source of milk, if external, is one breast or several, and if several, how to distinguish allies from enemies? Is this the good breast or the bad breast? Is it for me or against me? The earliest social interaction lays the basis for polarizing the world into classes. Survival depends on having enough emotional energy to carry this elementary classificatory enterprise through all the hard work needed to build a coherent, workable world. Social interaction supplies the element missing in the natural history account of the beginnings of classification.

Now the other half of the argument is stated. The intellectual requirements that must be met for social institutions to be stable are matched by social requirements for classification. Both are necessary for the foundations of a sociological epistemology; neither one is sufficient. The institution works as such when it acquires a third support from the harnessed moral energy of its members. More of this in the last chapter. All three processes are simultaneously at work. Individuals, as they pick and choose among the analogies from nature those they will give credence to, are also picking and choosing at the same time their allies and opponents and the pattern of their future relations. Constituting their version of nature, they are monitoring the constitution of their society. In short, they are constructing a machine for thinking and decision-making on their own behalf.

At this stage we can start to trace the effects of turning individual thought over to an automatic pilot. First, there is a saving of energy from institutional coding and inertia. The principle parallels a well-known characteristic of language. Frequent use makes some words hardy: not just the word but its declensions resist the syntactic developments that are happening all the time. Languages are in a constant state of change, but their most common words stand immune to the new inflections. For example, the common English word, man, with its archaic plural, men, has stood out against the onward sweep of plural endings in s. In the same way, the commonest social analogies are always there, resisting change. They stand ready to fill in gaps in causal chains when the demand for close reasoning is not strong enough to call forth complex classification. Thanks to the weight of institutional inertia, shifting images are held steady enough for communication to be possible.

Institutions bestow sameness. Socially based analogies assign disparate items to classes and load them with moral and political content. For example, the series that Lévi-Strauss has made familiar most recently in 1984, starts with nature distinguished from culture, and goes on to several levels. Elements on the same side of the taxonomy inevitably get classed together, males with culture, females with animality.

culture : nature
    human nature : animal nature
        male : female

And the submerged classification justifies a particular lot assigned
to women in the division of labor, whether as agricultural workers
and load carriers or as pretty little things incapable of thought. It
also justifies feminine behavior of spontaneity, easy tears, inconsistent wants, and nurturing care. Feminist theory in anthropology
has had a lot to say about these equations as justifying the subjec-
tion of women (Strathern 1980). Even when the feminine gender is
associated with the more esteemed side, it still can be used to
justify the women carrying the heaviest physical burdens. For
example, the men of Bamenda in Cameroon used to let their
women do all the heavy agricultural labor on the grounds that only
women and God could make things grow (Kaberry 1952).

The high values might be on the left or the right; the pattern
can be weighted for value in either direction. A modern Westerner
oriented to technology would weight the right side, and a funda-
mentalist Christian or Moslem would weight the left as the ideal in
the following set of matching pairs:

passivity	activity
permanence	change
antiquity	modernity

There are many instructive examples from the self-definition
of various professions. Economists are the strong theoreticians in
the social sciences. The institutions around them are based on
many relations of ordered pairs. Their own scheme of culture is
often portrayed as follows:

spiritual	material
poetry and religion	economics
speculative philosophy	applied science
vague metaphor	rigorous theory
intangibles	measurables
	economists

This set of analogies locates the scientific work with physical things, measurable facts, and scientific theories. When economists come, as they sometimes must, to determining a scale of human needs, they do not acknowledge that they have reached the limits of their professional competence. Instead of admitting parity with the layman, they go on speaking with professional authority, while relying on the instituted analogies of Western culture (Douglas and Isherwood 1979). This gives a hierarchical development of the spiritual : material opposition.

spiritual : physical
    luxuries (music, art) : necessities
        other needs (psychic) : primary needs (food, shelter)

The result is that policy makers and administrators pay attention to recurring deficits in food availability instead of to the balance of exchange entitlements through the whole society. According to A. K. Sen this results in disastrous decisions when a famine starts (Sen 1981).

Two examples have been used: the place of women in the world and the place of economists in the scheme of the professions. Each is chosen to illustrate how the division of labor supplies authority to an analogy that locates a structured social situation firmly in nature. As an analogy, it would have no immunity to the difficulties that beset natural kinds. Analogies can be seen anywhere and everywhere. But when an analogy matches a structure of authority or precedence, then the social pattern reinforces the logical patterns and gives it prominence. Two efforts, one social and one intellectual, mutually sustain each other. Patterns of authority or precedence enjoy a privileged status because, as Thomas Schelling has well said, their smallest indivisible parts are persons (Schelling 1978). A person cannot be divided, cannot be in two places at once, cannot be both superior and inferior within the same context, cannot have a cake and eat it. At some point there is an end to possible rearrangements of patterns involving persons. Patterns of authority or precedence are also privileged because we are social animals, trained from childhood to recognize the elementary materials of metaphor and analogy in our own social experience.

Like so much bric-a-brac, these proto-theoretical pieces lie around, ready to be pressed into service to promote the thinker's deepest social concerns or simply to be leaned upon and used whenever energy for independent classificatory work runs out Lévi-Strauss (1962) invented the image of the thinker as *bricoleur*, the amateur craftsman who turns the broken clock into a pipe rack, the broken table into an umbrella stand, the umbrella stand into a lamp, and anything into something else. The *bricoleur* uses everything there is to make transformations within a stock repertoire of furnishings. *Bricolage*, according to Lévi-Strauss, characterizes primitive thought. In a society where technology and the division of labor have been fixed at a certain level for generations, people can let their speculative thought run wild, but it cannot move beyond the limits set by the stable technology and the pattern of work. In a form of intellectual play what he has called the savage mind deploys the full range of witty parallels and inversions, with elaborate transformations on its stock of analogies. Lévi-Strauss accepts that intellectual *bricolage* is also found in modern society, but in nooks and crannies sheltered from pressure for change. Though he did not so extend it, his notion of bric-a-brac describes well the recurrent analogies and styles of thought that characterize any civilization.

Biological determinism is just such a recurring element in the intellectual history of the West. It is always available in one new form or another for proving that a wave of immigrants or an underclass is handicapped by its heredity, while the privileged have a happier physical makeup to transmit to their heirs (Gould 1981). For another example, gradualness over and over again has been pitted against sudden, discontinuous change; nature, God, and the Bible being invoked to support one or the other. The advocates of the status quo tend to find that nature is in favor of continuity; the advocates of radical reform read nature rather differently. Thus, even science, most carefully hedged from common political concerns by its terminology and training and segregated work places, shows the same tendency to found its institutions on analogies with nature and the same tendency to find the most general framework of its controversies corresponding to contemporary political debate. There is an ongoing argument about the value of urbanity versus rusticity, or, to put it the other way about, the city as a sink of iniquity versus the simplicity and goodness of rural life. This set of oppositions invoking nature

versus culture is constantly refurbished from the bric-a-brac remains of the last debate to provide natural analogies for whatever
new debate is politically to the fore.

As the construction of analogies from nature to support the
ongoing social system is well-known to anthropologists and others,
the novel points being made in this chapter need to be restated. It
is not usual to apply the idea of *bricolage* as a form of institutional
thinking to problems of rational choice. The two fields of inquiry,
symbolic anthropology and rational choice theory, are usually kept
well apart. Second, these points are worth making not only because they afford a new way of approaching collective action problems, but also because they change our way of thinking about
human cognition. The whole approach to individual cognition can
only benefit from recognizing the individual person's involvement
with institution-building from the very start of the cognitive enterprise. Even the simple acts of classifying and remembering are
institutionalized.

6

Institutions Remember and Forget

EVERY TEN YEARS OR so classroom text books go out of date. Their need to be revised is in some part due to new work in science or to the deeper delving of historians. Much more, it is because science has come to seem over-religious or scandalously irreligious (Nelkin 1977), or because the history of the last decade gives a wrong political feeling (Fitzgerald 1979). In the intervening years, some slogans have become risible, some words have become empty, and others too full, holding too much cruelty or bitterness to modern ears. Some names count for more, and others that count for less are due to be struck out. The revisionary effort is not aimed at producing the perfect optic flat. The mirror, if that is what history is, distorts as much after revision as it did before. The aim of revision is to get the distortions to match the mood of the present times. But the mirror is a poor metaphor of the public memory. The seeker after historical truth is not trying to get a clearer image of his own face, or even a more flattering image. Conscious tinkering and remaking is only a small part of the shaping of the past. When we look closely at the construction of past time, we find the process has very little to do with the past at all and everything to do with the present. Institutions create shadowed places in which nothing can be seen and no questions asked. They make other areas show finely discriminated detail, which is closely scrutinized and ordered. History emerges in an unintended shape as a result of practices directed to immediate, practical

69

ends. To watch these practices establish selective principles that highlight some kinds of events and obscure others is to inspect the social order operating on individual minds.

Public memory is the storage system for the social order. Thinking about it is as close as we can get to reflecting on the conditions of our own thought. We can trace the logical operations, but it is extremely difficult to think about them critically. Are we using an exhaustive set of the public categories on which the logical operations are performed? Are they the right categories for our questions? What does rightness of categories mean? And apart from those we have put into an analysis, what should we say about the ones we have left out? What about other social orders that might have been but did not come into existence? There is no way of directly confronting these questions. We can avoid insoluble riddles and still get an answer by examining the processes of public memory. Some patterns of public events get stored there, others get rejected.

The concept of structural amnesia arrived in British social anthropology in 1940 with the publication of Evans-Pritchard's book, *The Nuer* (1940). The fieldwork on which it was based belongs to the early 1930s. The anthropologist was already alerted to the relation between the social order and memory by the French school of *L'Année Sociologique* and particularly by Halbwachs' work on collective memory (1950). Of course, Marx and Hegel were there before. A dispute about prior discovery is no part of the intention of this chapter. It just happens that in the same period two contemporary thinkers converged on the same problem, treated it in very similar terms, and produced very comparable explanations. One is Evans-Pritchard and the other is Robert Merton, in sociology. Merton asked why scientists keep forgetting something that is very obvious and why they are so surprised when it is brought to their attention. That obvious thing is that science is a collective enterprise. The hard problems and good solutions have been bumping around together for centuries, and if someone makes a discovery he should not be astonished to learn that he is not the first; in one form or another it is almost certain to have been noticed already. In a long ironic essay, *On the Shoulders of Giants* (1965), Merton elaborates the pointlessness of asking who said a thing first. The best ideas and most famous quotations seem to have been around forever. Merton himself, so far from claiming priority, noted that Francis Bacon 350 years ago sketched the outline of a hypothesis to account for the multiple and independent rediscoveries of an idea.

Anthropologists tend to turn the question round. They are less inclined to ask why people forget. For them, remembering is the peculiar thing that needs to be explained. Anthropology has inherited an ancient criterion of intellectual advance based on the technology of war. Traditionally, the wonder has been that people with only primitive arrows for weapons ever remember anything at all. Technology is not such a bad criterion. There are engineering achievements that could not be performed before differential calculus was invented, and administrative triumphs that depend on double entry bookkeeping. Some basic techniques of discrimination, calculation, and holding in memory may be prerequisite for any particular form of knowledge. Anthropologists have always paid attention to the available counting skills. They have been especially fascinated by people who seem to do well without being able to count beyond three. Early writers were very interested in great feats of memory performed by people enjoying only a low level of technical competence. It was generally thought that rote learning was the secret (Bartlett 1932, Colby and Cole 1973). This fitted well with the assumption that real intellectual advances (presumably leading to more sophisticated weaponry) result from individuals being freed from institutional trammels. Yet this very assumption bears marks of severe trammelling, as we shall see in the next chapter.

Given their opposite formulations of the issue, the convergence of Robert Merton and Evans-Pritchard on the same solution is remarkable. One was intrigued to observe that multiple scientific discoveries were continually forgotten; the other was intrigued that out of unnumbered generations of ancestors, so many arrays of names should be securely fixed in memory. Both took the social system as their unit. Merton considered the systematic forgetting to be an integral part of the organization of science; Evans-Pritchard took the systematic remembering to be an integral part of the organization of a pastoral people in the Sudan. Which scientists and which ancestors get to be remembered is the same general question. Evans-Pritchard's study of how the cognitive processes of the Nuer are locked into their social institutions is a classic. In the context of their very simple technology, it is remarkable that they can generally recall nine to eleven generations of their ancestors. However do they remember all that when they only fight with spears and clubs? Closer study shows that they forget more than they remember. Their personal genealogies claim to run back to the beginning of time, but eleven generations do not at all cover even their history in the region. A lot of forgetting has been going on. Another curious fact is that despite the continual appearance of new generations, the number of known progenitors stays constant. Somewhere along the line a lot of ancestors are being dropped off the list. Somewhere after the tribal founder and his two sons and his four grandsons and his eight great grandsons, the tribal memory has developed a yawning hole, and multiple ancestors are tumbling headlong into it. They are not being forgotten randomly. The strengths and weaknesses of recall depend on a mnemonic system that is the whole social order. The Nuer study was an explicit demonstration of how institutions direct and control the memory. The following pages are summarized from three books by Evans-Pritchard (1940, 1951, 1956), which have been analyzed in another volume (Douglas 1980).

This is how it works. Among the Nuer the equivalent of a generally acceptable validating procedure is the fundamental equation: 40 head of cattle ratify a marriage. If they wavered on that fixed amount, transactions based upon its rightness would have to be renegotiated. Graded on this basis all other rights are computable. To reckon the right compensation for killing a man, the formula is extended: 1 woman and her progeny = 40 head of cattle = 1 man's life. Several legal fictions sprout from this basic formula. Under specified conditions, 1 woman = 1 man, so that a female link can be treated as a male one. Gaps and lumps in the genealogy are smoothed so that it presents an unbroken succession of males. A similar fiction allows a dead man to count as a legal father to a child begotten after his death. The Nuer rules of accounting allow flexibility without ambiguity or contradiction.

The Nuer public memory illustrates a principle of coherence: interlocking formulae of ratification ,make savings in cognitive energy. If we are interested in how some theories get their longevity, Fleck would have us note their service in private transactions. A few accepted procedures for making individual claims control a society's knowledge of its own past. Nuer marriages are nodal points in a regular pattern of exchange that sorts and collapses a variety of transactions into a uniform type of contract. Nuer have a good incentive to turn up at weddings and to work out in public their precise relationships. For a Nuer who goes to a wedding either expects to get a cow or will have to contribute a cow. Those who contributed to the groom's expenses will claim a cow when his daughter gets married a generation later. One of the cattle distributed at a marriage is allocated to a relative connected at the fifth generation, after which no further claims are recognized. Weddings and cattle distributions order the memory of the past up to the father's father's father in all directions—an impressive feat of memory if one had to do it alone, but the repeated patterns give plenty of incentive not to forget and their public assertion spreads the burden of remembering. Thus a set of names, such as the names of my father's father's father, his sisters and brothers, and their offspring, will not be lost if they are worked into the strategies for validating private claims.

A theory about how the world should be run will survive competition if it is more than a theory, for example, if it can intervene to support individual strategies to create a collective good. The Nuer theory of patrilineal descent does that service. The Nuer family depends on men for herding duties and on women for dairying; it needs to belong to a village. But recalling the problems of free-riding and the temptation to leave the collective tasks to be performed by everyone else, we should ask how the village can recruit men to conduct raids and to provide defense? The answer is, as a by-product of inheritance: young men can only get the cattle they need to marry with if they can prove links to the right ancestor. Inheritance compels them to make clear their group loyalty. Their political coalitions are based on the principle of descent from the four generations of the founding ancestor, his sons, grandsons, and great grandsons, each of whom founded a political unit. This level of their organization further prompts their memory of their ancestors. The top-down reckoning of political allegiance anchors the names of four to six remote generations. The strategy for making individual claims anchors five proximate generations on a reckoning from the bottom up. In between top down and bottom up lies the open gap into which successive generation of ancestors keep disappearing.

It is not merely that there is no special reason for remembering certain names, there is even strong pressure against it. The successful formula is predatory. Sheer consistency of use endows it with might, and it will swallow up competition.

The Nuer idea of ancestry has all these qualities. It also roots their knowledge in nature, for the ancestors go back to before the beginning of human society. It also matches well with their political feeling. The Nuer are fiercely egalitarian, individualistic, and independent. The disappearing ancestor trick puts everyone on a par with everyone else. It suits them not to know more about individual past history. If the political system that suited them had been a hereditary chieftaincy, they would have remembered more ancestors, or rather, certain of them would have. Royalty needs long lineage to vindicate dynastic claims.

Students of Evans-Pritchard developed the subject of institutionalized public memory by comparing social structures that could and could not sustain genealogical depth. The most fascinating part of that research lays bare the procedures by which genealogical history is clipped and stretched and smoothed out (Bohannon 1952, Barnes 1954). That early body of work stands in support of a trend in the sociology of science, the work on textbook writing that follows Merton on self-fulfilling prophecies (1949), and Thomas Kuhn on normal science (1962).

One reason why it was important to work step-by-step through these remote situations is to note the pragmatic effectiveness of the public memory. This should be enough to stop the invoking of a mystic cohesiveness for small-scale communities. A community works because the transactions balance out. The risk of free riding is controlled by the accounting system. The accounts are audited, and debts are collected by the way that God or nature punishes defaulters with disease and death. The thought style keeps the thought world in shape by directing its memory.

Let us now turn to physical scientists in our own society and observe their disbelief when confronted with historical facts that have not been entered into the public memory. Their angry repudiation of the possibility that another scientist could have found the same fact earlier or worked out the same theory first has drawn from Robert Merton a fine sociological analysis of an amnesic blind spot. This is described in a series of publications, starting with "Priorities in Scientific Discovery" (1957), "Singletons and Multiples in Scientific Discovery" (1962), and "Resistance to the Study of Multiple Discoveries in Science" (1963). The question is why the same fact with its associated hypotheses remains for decades and centuries "in a static condition, as though it were permanently condemned to repetition without extension," and then suddenly resurfaces.

The analysis shows that the star scientists, normally benign and generous, furiously deny a convergent or earlier discovery because their passions are driven by the way that science is organized. Merton links emotion, cognition, and social structure into one system. In science, the big rewards go to accredited innovation. The concept of original discovery is embedded in all the forms of institutional life, along with prizes and naming of plants, animals, measurements, and even diseases after scientists. The interpersonal relations of scientists are governed by an institutionalized competition in which everyone loses something: otherwise magnanimous scholars are belittled by their own destructive anger when they learn of a competitor to their claim to be first; they are baffled to meet discordant facts that do not fit their categories; the profession loses from practices of secrecy, which contradict intellectual openness; and science policy is misled by the fallacy that duplication is avoidable and wasteful. Standing coolly outside the rivalry, Merton shows how a distinctive social order generates its pattern of values, commits the hearts of its members, and creates a myopia which certainly seems to be inevitable. Because Merton is not a physical scientist, he can think thoughts about their social order that are impossible for insiders. After he has described the blinders they wear, we can ask how those scientists could possibly give credit to the idea of multiple discoveries? Even when told about such discoveries, how could they ever keep them in mind? Scientists' thoughts are held in the grip of the exacting institution of science, as ours are held in other institutions. They cannot reflect calmly upon it, and nor can we. We need a technique for standing aside from our own society, developing Merton's little cybernetic model into a big one with several compartments that deal with the passions inherent in different forms of social organization and that display the control which socially reinforced motivations have upon individual vision.

A good functionalist argument does not need to invoke a pathological state to explain forgetting. In 1957 Merton regarded the resistance to multiple discoveries as the normal response to a badly integrated institution. Using Freudian terms, he defined the resistance as motivated denial of an accessible but painful reality. In later writings, that part of the argument has been dropped. It is more instructive to expect the peculiar effects of a competitive social organization upon memory to be functional than dysfunctional. Certain things always need to be forgotten for any cognitive system to work. There is no way of paying full attention to everything.

Note that Merton has made a back-door approach to the problem. He is not asking "How do people think about the constraints the social order imposes on their thought?" He asks "How are they prevented from thinking? What are the impossible thoughts?" He shows what thoughts are discarded by the system. This is another clue to how we might do well to proceed. Back-door approaches to difficult questions can be formulated in a way that escapes the self-referencing dilemma. Ask people what foods they eat and they will answer what they think you think they ought to eat. A team of Arizona nutritionists once imitated the archeologists by getting their information from domestic garbage heaps (Rathje 1975). The food rejects tell more surely about the diet than answers to questionnaires. The theory of social deviance is another kind of back-door approach to cognitive sociology: it examines the rejects. Too much interpretation can be put upon positive statements about what behavior is most honored. Much clearer evidence comes from studying aversion. The rules for avoiding reprehensible behavior and the punishing and purifying after disapproved contact are more clearly known and easier to elicit (Douglas 1966). A sociological theory of rejection can be more securely based than a sociological theory of value because of the public nature of penalties and prohibitions which follow on negative attitudes. The same is true for our problem. The thinkability of the social order is beset with infinite regress. Institutional influences become apparent through a focus on unthinkables and unmemorables, events that we can note at the same time as we observe them slipping beyond recall.

Once a social system has been founded in reason and nature, we can see how cognitive energy is saved by tracing the career of a successful theory. First, on the principle of cognitive coherence, a theory that is going to gain a permanent place in the public repertoire of what is known will need to interlock with the procedures that guarantee other kinds of theories. At the foundation of any large cognitive enterprise are some basic formulae, equations in common use, and rules of thumb. In science such shared techniques of validating spread across different subdisciplines. For example, the mathematics of seepage is used in minerology and in ophthalmology. So also the Nuer use the same formula for marriage and blood debts. The anchoring of a set of theories in one field imparts authority to a set elsewhere, if it can be anchored by the same procedures. This is just as true for social forms of validation as for scientific ones.

Forgotten ancestors and forgotten scientific discoveries are in the same case. Scientific precursors disappear from view because they never had an earthly chance of making their way to the surface of public memory. Forgotten discoverers are like a lot of forgotten ancestors. The pattern of their failure is not random. The strategies to validate scientists' claims use originality as a main criterion for prizes and positions. The belief in a first discoverer is nothing without the prizes and renown. The custom of naming immediately gives a major advantage to claimed originality and a disadvantage to the fact of rediscovery. What seems dysfunctional when enraged scientists make a public display of their vanity may be counted as the cost of keeping the race open to the swift. But competition is always costly in human terms. In such an environment, the principle of rediscovery has no strong qualifications for being remembered. Most rediscovered theories turn out not to have built originally on the current cognitive infrastructure and so to have missed savings in energy. Often when a new scientific discovery has been rejected and left to lie inert until later, it is precisely an idea which lacked formulaic interlocking with normal procedures of validation. The best chance of success is to confront the major public concerns and to exploit the major analogies on which the socio-cognitive system rests.

The Nuer example does more for the social theory of memory than does the example of the scientists. The institutionalized memory of the Nuer explains not just that some ancestors will be remembered, but which ones are set for posterity and which will disappear, and after how many generations. It illustrates the point about political sensitivity as well as dependence on accepted techniques of validation. The instance of the name-conscious scientists depends for its explanatory value only on the lack of fit between the conventions of the naming system and the real situation of shared knowledge. This suggests that the argument of this chapter relies too much on an exotic example. Another modern case is needed apart from that of the scientists to illustrate the influence of the wider social environment and of the existing validating techniques.

Kenneth Arrow has described his own discovery of a difficulty in the concept of social welfare (1984). Note that this discovery, his impossibility theorem, itself lay inactive on the shelf, arousing the interest of only a few persons for some twenty years, and then it suddenly became one of the dominating concepts of political science in the West. His personal biography starts with a childhood in the depression, a student interest in economic planning and in logic and coherence; he was attracted by the assumption of general equilibrium theory that every economic activity is connected with every other one. He started with the mathematics of consumer indifference maps and applied it to the theory of the firm. What if the firm had many owners instead of the single owner postulated by the theory? And suppose they had different expectations of the future? Then they would have different preferences over investment plans. Suppose they tried to reach a decision by voting? Then it quickly became clear that majority voting did not necesarily lead to an ordering. From here his mind turned in 1948 to the political context where majority voting was the normal way of settling differences. Within a month he found the same perception of the problem published by Duncan Black in the *Journal of Political Economy* (1948). Then he was led to recognizing a parallel for problems in international relations. Surveying such a broad spectrum of behavior under one rubric, from economics to national politics to the international scene, he was able to make the confident generalization: neither the majority vote nor any other way of aggregating preferences would work to define an ordering. So he formulated the conditions under which it is impossible to aggregate individual preferences.

Of course, he was seeing from the shoulders of giants. Of course, he was benefiting from the existing mathematical procedures. The mystery is not how he arrived at his theorem, or how he and Black converged on it in the same year. The mystery that he chose to comment on is why J. C. de Borda's discovery in 1781 and why Condorcet's formulation of the same discovery in 1785 had been so completely forgotten (Condorcet 1785). Arrow says that when he first realized that majority voting would not necessarily lead to an ordering:

> I was convinced that what we presently call the Condorcet paradox was not new. I am at a loss to identify the source of my belief, now that I know the previous literature, since I could not possibly have seen any of this obscure material prior to

> 1946 . . . unlike some other examples of multiple discovery, this one still surprises me. The mathematics after all could have been carried out by Condorcet, and there had been no active body of literature raising comparable questions. (Arrow 1984, p. 129)

Condorcet's discovery was buried for 160 years. Then in 1948 and 1949 two papers by Black and in 1951 Kenneth Arrow's monograph appeared.

> Neither Black nor I were aware at the time we first wrote of the preceding literature. (Arrow 1984, p. 129)

The explanation for Condorcet's discovery having been forgotten is not that the mathematical apparatus available in the eighteenth century was inadequate. It is the different climate of ideas, political and philosophical, in which he worked out his proof. For Condorcet the object of the theory of voting was to find the true opinion, the right social choice independent of the wishes of the voters. The effect of making a decision by voting was to find an authoritative solution. The role of the voters was to express their degree of understanding of the truth being sought. He considered the kind of tradeoffs that would be made by having a large number of voters, some of whom were ignorant but at least able to bring to bear a wide range of experience, as against a few specialists with more knowledge per head. His discovery was that with more than two alternatives and more than two votes it was possible to get a circular ordering, such that no alternative could satisfy a majority of the electorate.

When it is recognized that a majority could prefer A to B, and B to C, but C to A, confidence in the will of something called "the majority" is eroded.

But why would this discovery be important at all in the eighteenth century? The recondite mathematics of circular voting hardly mattered in a country about to go up in revolution, and later the actual message of the theory would hardly be welcome to nineteenth century politicians whose concern was to extend the franchise and to limit elitist political control. It must still be heard as bad news by those with a simple faith in majority decisions. The liberal consensus is based on the Benthamite principle that the

greatest happiness of the greatest number is a unique and mean-
ingful result. The theory only becomes relevant to political science
at the end of the twentieth century when the franchise is universal
and can no more be extended, when pluralism makes a political
consensus harder to achieve, and when questioning is rife about
the foundations of democratic society. A new discovery has to be
compatible with political and philosophical assumptions if it is to
get off the ground in the first place, to say nothing of being remembered afterwards. It is not enough to keep repeating that memory
is socially structured. To have come so far invites a further step.
The next thing is to discover what qualities of institutional life
have distinctive effects on remembering.

Just as each different kind of social system rests on a specific
type of analogy from nature, so the memories ought to be different
too. As Merton's example shows, competitive social systems are
weaker on memory than ascriptive ones. This must be so because
the competition drives out some players and brings upstarts to the
top, and with each change of dynasty, public memory necessarily
gets rearranged. By contrast, complex hierarchical society will
need to recall many reference points in the past. But the list of
founding fathers will only be as long as the list of social units they
have founded. Peace treaties will be benchmarks assigning relative
status to incorporated enemies. In so far as there is pressure toward coherent principles of organization, so will the justificatory
stories of the past be amalgamated and rationalized as part of the
social process. Coherence and complexity in public memory will
tend to correspond to coherence and complexity at the social level.
This is what Halbwachs taught. The converse follows: the more the
social units are simple and isolated, the simpler and more frag-
mentary the public memory will be, with fewer benchmarks and
fewer levels of ascent to the beginning of time (Rayner 1982). The
more the social organization is a latent group, conscious of the
organizational problems detailed in chapter three, the more its
members will invoke a history of persecution and resistance. The
competitive society celebrates its heroes, the hierarchy celebrates
its patriarchs, and the sect its martyrs.

7

A Case of Institutional Forgetting

WEAK OR STRONG, memory is sustained by institutional structures. The scientists, mathematicians, and pastoralists mentioned in the last chapter are very specialized kinds of communities. The question hits nearer to home if we turn to the case of an eminent psychologist who specialized on remembering. Frederick Bartlett fully intended to study institutional effects on cognition. His own institution diverted him from the project. According to the thought style of his day, it was improbable that institutional constraints would have much influence on moderns, so it would not be worth searching for them. And in any case, the experimental conditions in which he worked were not able to capture institutional effects. His career is a self-referencing instance of the claim that psychologists are institutionally incapable of remembering that humans are social beings. As soon as they know it, they forget it. They often remind one another of how artificial the parameters are that they have set around their subject matter. Famous psychologists keep upbraiding their fellows for despising or ignoring institutional factors in cognition. The literature of the social sciences is sprinkled with rediscoveries of that very idea.

Leon Festinger wrote in 1948 on the relation between the spread of information and the degree of integration in a group. Some measure of integration could have become the basis of a number of theories about the relation between knowledge and society, but nothing was done about it.

James Coleman is another who was prominent in making efforts in the 1950s to treat qualities of the social situation as selective principles for acceptable information. Comparing doctors' judgments on medical innovation, he and his colleagues found that doctors who were in an integrated professional network made decisions to adopt or not to adopt a new drug more quickly than more isolated practitioners. This research was expected to inaugurate a new approach in social research, in which social relationships and social structures would be the units of analysis. Coleman anticipated that the new approach would focus on the fate of information transmitted through more integrated and less integrated social networks (Coleman 1957). However, network analysis has proceeded without bringing the parallel and necessary analysis of attitudes and values to the same heights of sophistication, and no systematic synthesizing theory has been developed.

More recently, J. M. F. Jaspers writes about the use made in cognitive psychology of the concept of attitudes. He discovers that the social nature of attitudes has been completely overlooked. He traces the current increase of dissatisfaction with attitude research:

> We have lost sight of the collective nature of attitudes because attitudes have been impounded by social psychology and made into individual response dispositions of an evaluative nature. . . . Recent developments in attitude research and scaling techniques have led to a complete individualization of the study of attitude. (Jaspers and Frazer 1981, p. 116)

There must be hundreds more of such isolated complaints, insights, and independent discoveries. They have been doomed. There is a professional dislike of control models, which inevitably smack of social engineering, sociological determinism, and Big Brother's 1984 apotheosis. In 1975 Donald Campbell put his finger on the spot. Psychologists, he said, are so committed to the assumption that individual psychic development is restricted by social conventions that they see all conventional and institutional constraints as wrongful. He makes the psychologists sound like a romantic band of knights errant seeking to deliver the weak and infirm from the illegitimate claims imposed by life and society. For psychologists, the idea that stabilizing factors could be useful for cognitive and emotional development is unthinkable. Campbell says in so many words that it is professionally impossible in psychology to establish the notion that institutional constraints can be beneficial to the individual. The notion can be scouted, but it cannot enter the memorable corpus of facts. To counteract this bias he strongly recommended that institutional sources of stability be given priority in research (Campbell 1975). But then he proved his point by instantly forgetting his good advice. Now he is seeking stabilizing factors in our biological makeup. However, his finger is pointing to the one idea we must explore to understand why our self-knowledge is so elusive. This idea is that the burden of thinking is transferred to institutions. His own case suggests it is an inherently unstable idea, and we should surely expect as much, given what we know already about the difficulties of a self-reflexive program of inquiry. However, since it is important, we could start by going more deeply into the sources of its weakness.

Sir Frederick Bartlett was born in 1886 and became Director of the Cambridge Psychology Laboratory and longtime editor of the *British Journal of Psychology*. His research and teaching successfully established a major insight: the importance of selective and constructive elements in human awareness. That was only half of what he set out to do. The other half remained undone.

When Bartlett first went to St. John's College, W. H. R. Rivers was there, a very influential anthropologist, physiologist, and psychologist. Rivers had been editor of the *British Journal of Psychology* from 1904 to 1913. He had been a member of the great Cambridge expedition to the Torres Straits in 1898, along with other famous psychologists and doctors, including C. S. Myers, William McDougall, and C. S. Seligman. The object of the expedition was to make a many-fronted study of the evolution of human cognition based on the population of Melanesia. The team was led by A. C. Haddon, originally a marine biologist, then a Melanesian ethnologist and specialist on the evolution of primitive art.

Bartlett always claimed his own research was deeply influenced by Rivers and by Haddon, two anthropologists. From Rivers he adopted the idea that individual emotions and cognition are institutionalized in social forms. From Haddon's work on Melanesian art he adopted the idea that an experimental study of cognition should focus on the process of standardization or conventionalization. In 1913 he was actually under contract to Cambridge University Press to write a book on conventionalization. I believe that both these intentions were doomed from the outset.

The reader may be hard to convince that this established psychologist was ever looking for a sociological theory of perception. Most of the evidence depends on the use made by Bartlett of Rivers' *Instinct and the Unconscious* (1920). Rivers was imbued with the idea that the development of the individual and the development of society followed the same evolutionary process. He presented a theory of mind that was also a theory of society. His intellectual training had been in medicine and experimental psychology. He published on vision, fatigue, optical illusions, the effects of drugs, and other factors affecting consciousness. At the same time he was very much the expeditionary field anthropologist, having gone to Melanesia in 1898, to India in 1902, and to Oceania in 1908 and 1914. The quest for human instincts and the placing of instincts into patterns of culture were abiding sources of speculation for Rivers. His technique for relating the individual to society was simply to use a single developmental model into whose slots either could be fitted, finding parallels between the relations of higher and lower levels.

He was mature in his thought and already thirty-nine years old when he joined the celebrated neurologist, Henry Head, in research on the nervous system. In a famous experiment, Head offered his own arm, a surgeon made incisions on it, and Rivers asked questions about the sensations at different points and recorded Head's answers. Given his strong commitment to the theory of evolution, it is not surprising that Rivers' description of the experiment (in *Brain* 1908) showed it to have rich evolutionary implications. The research, which became paradigmatic for Rivers' later writings, reported the discovery of two kinds of sensory nerves. One, which Rivers and Head called punctate protopathic sensibility, gave an all or nothing response. It occurred at a lower level of neural organization. It had diffuse localizing functions. Cut those nerves and the subject becomes less able to say yes or no about his sensation and its limits, but even with those nerves intact he still cannot precisely say where the pain hurts. At a higher organizational level, the other kind of sensory nerves, which Rivers and Head called the refined epicritic sensibility, was capable of finely graded discriminations and accurate localizing. In the same report Rivers suggested a way to build an evolutionary model showing mankind's development from an inherited or instinctual nervous system dominated by the protopathic function at the primitive stage, to a system gradually moving with the advance of evolution to being under the control of the epicritic function.

Evading any tough technical analysis, Rivers was able to float around, seeming to believe in the inheritance of acquired characteristics and certainly never risking any theory to account for the alleged evolutionary transformation of human beings. He was successful in his generation because instead of an analytic tool he had a magic wand that he used to vanquish his opponents and to develop fashionably acceptable metaphors of mind and society. The favorite metaphor, which recurs in everything he wrote, is a model of control in the nervous system extended to control of the mind and extended to social control. He explains it very clearly in *Dreams and Primitive Culture* (1918) where he compares the mechanism of dream production in individuals with the mechanism of myth production in primitive culture (always acknowledging his debt to the genius of Freud). The primitive generally comes out of the comparison poorly. Primitive peoples are representatives of earlier infantile stages of human progress (Rivers 1918, p. 406). This is institutional thinking with a vengeance and a fine example for our collection of bric-a-brac. The model is a two-tier box, with a small section on top, where the epicritic nervous function controls the protopathic instincts. He fits the life cycle development of the human individual into the same box, with order and reason in the top box and disorderly emotions in the bottom one. The model also applies to a contrast between logical thinking at the top and dreams and myths in the lower box. It applies to civil society, with sovereign institutions of control at the top, chaotic riot and revolution at the bottom. It applies to colonial administrators (top box) attempting to control natives (bottom box). In an appendix added in 1922 Rivers adapted Freud's conception of censorship to both the nervous system and the social system, all within an evolutionary framework. He taught that each was arranged so "far as function is concerned, in a number of levels, one above the other, forming a hierarchy in which each level controls those beneath it and is itself controlled by those above" (Rivers 1922, p. 229). Rivers assumed that the life history of a human psyche develops a similar hierarchy of controls over unconscious experience. Hysteria was to be explained by a process that puts the higher levels into abeyance and gives free rein to the lower, instinctual levels. This is very close to the current model of growth to moral maturity still credited in developmental psychology. But Rivers was quite explicit about his commitment to an evolutionary theory and he also tried to add the social dimension.

Bartlett did not accept the full legacy of Rivers' ideas or keep them intact. For example, Rivers' cybernetic idea of the relation between psyche and society is strongly authoritarian. When Bartlett wrote *Psychology and the Soldier* (1927), he based it on Rivers' *Instinct and the Unconscious* and used Rivers' main terms—instincts, group tendencies, and inhibitory mechanisms—but reaching toward a feedback theory of the relation between individual and society, he democratized the model to show that control may be consensual (Bartlett 1927, p. 113).

In his earlier book, *Psychology and Primitive Culture* (1923), Bartlett had taught emphatically that the individual is always a social individual and that social influences selectively control cognition and emotion. He was already drawing heavily on Rivers' work and comparing something he and Rivers called "primitive comradeship" with the "collective conscience" of the writers of the *L'Année Sociologique*. He described how in primitive society conflict is averted by instituted separation—a pregnant idea—and how curiosity is brought under institutional control.

One reason why this interest in institutional control on thinking never became more than a speculation lies undoubtedly in certain current evolutionary assumptions. Both Bartlett and Rivers thought (along with Durkheim) that social control of the free ranging curiosity of individuals was stronger in primitive society. The primitive individual was altogether less of an individual and more of an automaton obeying group cues. This evolutionary assumption was quite congenial to the period of colonial empire and provided the latter with its naturalizing analogies. It was self-evident that modern man had lost his natural sensitivity to group signals, just as the human race had lost the sense of smell so useful in lower animal orders. Another contemporary assumption was that visual memory was also a relic of a less evolved stage of the human mind. Freud was generally supposed not to have used his visual imagination, and he designated Charcot as *un type visuel* with a hint of disparagement (Lewin 1969, p. 7). William James had noted a life cycle tendency to lose the capacity to visualize. He was probably not joking when he said:

> The older men are and the more effective as thinkers, the more, as a rule, they have lost their visualizing power . . . This was ascertained by Mr. Galton to be the case with members of the Royal Society. (James 1890, vol. 1, p. 266)

Raymond Firth (1968) remarks that Rivers claimed many times to have weak visual imagery. But he certainly did not feel deprived.

> Often the images by which the dream-thoughts are expressed are much more vivid than those of waking life, while persons in whom sensory imagery is almost or wholly absent when awake may see and hear the occurrences of a dream as definitely as if they formed part of real life. Similarly there is reason to believe that sensory imagery is more vivid and necessary to the savage than to civilized persons . . . among savage peoples . . . [there is] almost exclusive interest in the concrete, with the high degree of development of their powers of observation and with the accuracy and fulness of memory of the more concrete details. (1920, p. 396)

Bartlett's account of memory among contemporary African peoples suggests a mysterious osmotic process quite unlike what he took to be the pure ratiocination of moderns (Bartlett 1932), but rather akin to the mystical process invoked by those who believe that smallness of scale in itself solves problems of collective action. Since this quasi-instinctual faculty was in his opinion less well-adapted to modern life, Bartlett tacitly exonerated himself from trying to study it, though he continued to the end emphasizing the importance of the social input to perception.

So much for Rivers' influence on Bartlett's sociological interests. Now we turn to Haddon, the other anthropologist whom Bartlett especially acknowledged. Haddon's work on conventionalization in Melanesian art influenced Bartlett's choice of research site. The power of cultural convention to control perception and recall was initially Bartlett's prime problem. He wanted to discover how attention is directed. He expected that the perceptual processes of the individual are linked to the individual's deepest emotions and these, according to Rivers, are determined by the form of institutions. Bartlett seems to have been on the verge of a nervous collapse trying to write his promised book on conventionalization. He had read all the gestalt work on memory and decided that the German psychologists could go no further along the route they were pursuing. He wanted to experiment on perception of a whole, instead of experimenting on the faculty of memory exercised on jumbled nonsense. James Ward had advised him to research sequences of perceptions (Bartlett 1932, p. 63). But clearly he was stalled for a long time while searching for an experimental design.

In 1913, Norbert Wiener, then aged nineteen with a doctorate in philosophy from Harvard University, came to Cambridge to work with Bertrand Russell. Bartlett confided his research block to the young man, and Wiener suggested the experimental method which was to make Bartlett famous: the method of serial reproduction of "Russian scandal." The technique was to use perceptual sequences with some element missing from or added to a pattern and then to score how the observers "constructed a terminating design before they had reached it and reported having seen detail which in fact was not there" (Bartlett 1958, p. 142). This research enabled him to demonstrate conclusively the active organizing of perception by the perceiver. But it was designed so that it never could discover or assess the social influences that direct attention.

Bartlett became a great designer of experiments. We can read how they became more and more strict, subtle, and amenable to objective scoring. The design of the research focused, true enough, on the process of conventionalization, but River's original hypothesis about institutional influence could never be tested. Experimental stringency required the particular differences of emotional interest affecting each subject to be strictly excluded. The social dimension of their experience was peeled away from the subjects. Broadbent, who wrote the notice of Bartlett in the *Dictionary of National Biography* (1970), recorded that Bartlett's special contribution to psychology was to show perception and remembering to be controlled by some process sensitive to the purposes and interests of the perceiver. But all the ambitions Bartlett had earlier expressed about analyzing the selective process were frustrated. His story is full of ironies. The expert on memory had himself managed to forget his own teachings. He who taught that intentions guide cognition, forgot his own intentions. Looking for a cybernetic system, he had the extraordinary luck to meet the future inventor of cybernetics. Something was always happening to distract his vision. Those fragile good ideas fell into the waters of oblivion, waiting for the next phase in the cycle of rediscovery.

If we run his forgotten discovery through our four-fold prescription for a successful fact, we find it was wrecked on the first requirement. There was not and never has been since a way of latching his insight about institutionalized selective principles onto the accepted formulae of psychological research. The analytic tools that Rivers bequeathed to him were about as sharp as jelly. Those ideas of Bartlett that did succeed exploited an existing set of tools. He would not have needed greatly to change C. S. Myers' chapter on statistical method in *A Textbook of Experimental Psychology* (1911) to carry out his work. The analysis of variance, already powerful in other branches of psychology, demography, sociology, and economics, was there at hand and becoming increasingly sophisticated. One well-instituted tool can easily ruin the career of a theory that cannot use it. One well-connected unifying method can drive out an idea that does not depend upon its accredited formula. At a narrow professional level Bartlett's contribution was completely positive. However, the loss of his initial insight about the social control of cognition has been counterproductive for our understanding of cognition as well as of the social fabric.

Who would seriously maintain that it is wrong for sociology to try to develop a systematic approach to social factors influencing cognition? The assumptions that underpin our sociological theorizing impinge too heavily on this topic for it to be brushed aside as trivial. It seems fair enough for the applied disciplines, such as market research, to think off the top of their heads about connections between attitudes and social pressures. It even seems fair enough for the economists to leave motivations to other specialists—but to whom if not to the sociologists? After all, this is about socially structured forgetting. The burden of proof lies on those who maintain that a vast amount of work on this very subject exists. If the problem is well known, active steps are not being taken to remedy it. Spot research that connects one social factor to one kind of bias does not qualify, nor does research that shows local blank areas in cognition. It is true that there is a lot of that kind of inquiry without a sustained theoretical scheme; plenty of research embarks on this very problem without identifying a bounded social system as Merton identified a system of science organization and as anthropologists identify a social group. The failed theory in question would seek to connect the social order in a systematic way with the cognitive processes of its members.

Only one term sums up all the qualities that enable a speculation to become established and then to escape oblivion; that is the principle of coherence. To employ the same interlocking methodology that holds other clumps of scientific activity together is essential. With this secure, much else will be added; individual researchers will know how to ratify their private claims and how to attract collaborators to collective action; they will know what can safely be overlooked and what must be remembered.

The principle of coherence is not satisfied by purely cognitive and technological fit. It must also be founded on accepted analogies with nature. This means that it needs to be compatible with the prevailing political values, which are themselves naturalized. Nineteenth-century science received great stimulus to research whenever scientists saw in their work a grand analogy that matched nature. Inevitably, if it seems that an analogy does match nature, it is because the analogy is already in use for grounding dominant political assumptions. It is not nature that makes the match, but society. Ernst Haeckel's theory that the tree of life (Gould 1981, p. 114) might be read from the embryological development of higher forms led to wide speculative experimentation with the idea of "recapitulation," what Gould has called one of the most influential ideas of the late nineteenth century (1981). Gould notes that Freud and Jung were convinced recapitulationists and that Herbert Spencer lent his authority to the claim that "the intellectual traits of the uncivilized . . . are the traits recurring in children of the civilized . . . women's body and soul is phyleticaly older and more primitive . . . while man is more modern" (Gould 1981, pp. 89–90). If Rivers had a great success for his colonial model of psychic control and if Bartlett neglected the project of identifying social pressures on the cognition of modern man, both the success of the one and the diversion of the other's intent can be explained by the power of a dominant naturalizing metaphor. The metaphor of evolutionary progress in nature was so congenial that any research based on it could claim the benefits of general coherence.

8

Institutions Do the Classifying

WHEN THE INSTITUTIONS make classifications for us, we seem to lose some independence that we might conceivably have otherwise had. This thought is one that we have every reason, as individuals, to resist. Living together, we take individual responsibility and we lay it upon one another. We take responsibility for our deeds, but even more voluntarily for our thoughts. Our social interaction consists very much in telling one another what right thinking is and passing blame on wrong thinking. This is indeed how we build the institutions, squeezing each other's ideas into a common shape so that we can prove rightness by sheer numbers of independent assent. So much is this claim to intellectual independence recognized as a basis of our social life that moral philosophy takes its stand at that very point. This is why Durkheim's idea that the social group acts like one mind is so repugnant.

The judgment of history covers a paradox here. The more an influential thinker can be shown to have been repeating the favorite slogans of his times, the more scathingly he will be denounced for that very cause in the next generation. His resounding greatness was a mere echo of what everyone else was saying. He was not original but a copyist. He should have stood against the times. He was a mere reed, a passive instrument on which the spirit of the age blew its tune. The scorn is particularly laden with moral judgments; it was not to his credit to supinely join the latest shift of opinion on slavery, insanity, eugenics, or colonial empire. This is the easiest posture of moral superiority to adopt because the critic of past institutions is helping the nascent institutional structures of his day to mount their own defense against the past. This is the Marxist critique of reason, which often results in historical relativism. Each period is marked by its own thought style tailored to the concerns of the dominant class. At each period, a particular story of mankind drowns out other multiple, contradictory versions. In this same critical spirit, in his archaeology of Western thought, Michel Foucault attacked all significant institutions, showing how they straitjacket minds and bodies (1970). He showed how thought is translated directly into institutions, or vice versa, how institutions overcome individual thought and trim the body's shape to their conventions.

But an institution cannot have purposes. This we saw in the criticisms of Fleck's essay on the genesis of a fact. Only individuals can intend, plan consciously, and contrive oblique strategies. To retain its force Foucault's insight has to be taken a stage further. At the point of relevation, when the spurious sovereignty of a past thought style is demonstrated, critical opinion has lost its ground unless it can find a way of distinguishing the influence of the current thought style on its own thought and still justify its own judgment. Institutions systematically direct individual memory and channel our perceptions into forms compatible with the relations they authorize. They fix processes that are essentially dynamic, they hide their influence, and they rouse our emotions to a standardized pitch on standardized issues. Add to all this that they endow themselves with rightness and send their mutual corroboration cascading through all the levels of our information system. No wonder they easily recruit us into joining their narcissistic self-contemplation. Any problems we try to think about are automatically transformed into their own organizational problems. The solutions they proffer only come from the limited range of their experience. If the institution is one that depends on participation, it will reply to our frantic question: "More participation!" If it is one that depends on authority, it will only reply: "More authority!" Institutions have the pathetic megalomania of the computer whose whole vision of the world is its own program. For us, the hope of intellectual independence is to resist, and the necessary first step in resistance is to discover how the institutional grip is laid upon our mind.

The social theory of Max Weber and that of Durkheim illustrate respectively the mixed advantages of leaving institutions to
do their own classifying (Weber), and the difficulties of inspecting
how they do it (Durkheim). Weber has had much more influence
than Durkheim. He set the terms for thinking about modernism
and postmodernism. His success is mainly due to the large canvas
on which he synthesized what was already the thinking of his
generation. He offered intellectuals of his day a vision of the history of other great civilizations in terms of their own familiar
institutions. Both Durkheim and Weber focused their inquiry on
rationality and specifically on the relation between ideas and institutions. For both the main interest was the emergence of individualism as a philosophical principle. In Durkheim's case the task
was to explain the general question of individual commitment to
the social order—the issue of solidarity, which is the same as
collective action. He found the answer in shared classification.
Durkheim's work on the social origin of classification affords an
independent method of self-inspection. It provides a technique for
analysis that could be made proof against institutional distortion.
For Weber, the task was to explain the prevalence of particular
ideas and ideals at a particular stage of institutional development.
These remarks already show that Durkheim had placed his inquiry
at a higher level of abstraction. In Weber's time the instituted
intellectual options were either a Hegelian type of idealism (difficult and implausible given the climate of opinion in sociology), or a
Marxist type of sociological determinism. He chose a middle path
between idealism and determinism. For the monumental contribution he made to the understanding of rationality and institutional
forms, he left no systematic method to his followers for analyzing
the relation more finely. He left them a pile of trouble about what
he really meant by the spirit of Protestantism or the spirit of the
age.
    Weber's basic model of society is an equilibrium between
different institutional sectors. His main explanation for change is
the description of historical forces making for disequilibrium. Secular thought divides into two sectors, one dominated by market
institutions and the other by bureaucracy. The market rationality
is characterized by means-ends individual practical reasoning;
bureaucratic rationality is characterized by institutional thinking,
that is, abstraction and routinization. Weber's dichotomy still
dominates political theory and has imparted an unshiftable bias to

our habitual ways of thinking about organizations (see Douglas 1986). In religious sociology Weber makes the distinction between religious and secular life. He hives off religious from secular behavior and puts it into a institutional compartment of its own. Weber's classification of religion always follows the traditional classification of religious roles, which is part of the regular, real life differentiation of religious institutions. A thinker who classifies the phenomena to be examined according to known and visible institutions saves himself the trouble of justifying the classification. It is already the normal conceptual scheme for those who live in and think through similar institutions. But in doing this, Weber foists a tangled problem on religious sociology. Since religion has been defined institutionally and secularization has been defined by disengagement of religions from institutions, secularization implies a net loss for religion. However, withdrawal of religious life from secular institutions can happen without a loss of private faith. Gain in private faith and loss of public ceremony do not happen necessarily in the same process, as many commentators have pointed out. In displaying the religious history of Israel, China, and India, Weber uses the institutional framework of Western society. This enables him to draw on our current idea of our historical experience, instead of calling on any causal theory of change. In the panorama of great civilizations each starts in a primitive community (which remains unexamined). They all move thereafter at different periods through the same stages: a feudal one in which the equivalent of nobles are distinguishable from equivalents of peasantry and from which an emergent commercial sector will eventually shift the whole system to an urban scene. The beginning is veiled with sacredness and wonder; urbanization introduces markets, intelligentsia, bureaucracy, priesthood, and also pariah groups. The urban institutions will grow and converge to the point that we now experience and deplore. The story concludes with tearing down of veils, loss of enchantment, questioning, and the end of legitimacy. The unlikely tale proposed by such institutional thinking is that legitimacy has ever existed unquestioned anywhere. That there was once a period of unquestioned legitimacy is the idea that our institutions use for stigmatizing subversive elements. By this astute ploy, the idea is given that incoherence and doubt are new arrivals, along with tramcars and electric light, unnatural intruders upon primeval trust in the idyllic small community. Whereas it is more plausible that human history is studded all the way from the beginning with nails driven into local coffins of authority.

Weber's regret at the passing of the childhood of mankind is sweetened by exaltation. The modern takeoff into intellectual freedom means the challenge of a grown-up world without priestcraft or magic or other tyranny. The new fears, terrifying as they may be, are real fears, not false superstitions; they entail real responsibilities and real privileges, not illusions. Weber's sociological golden dawn is a counterpart of Frazer's mythological golden bough and of River's colonial model of the psyche (1920). If they spoke in chorus, it was because the same institutions were doing their thinking.

In the introduction to *The Protestant Ethic* (1905), Weber said he read as much as he could to present the argument as clearly as he could, but he apologized for having neglected ethnography. In the context it certainly seems a very minor omission. How could those small exotic tribes, that so intrigued Durkheim and Mauss, have any relevance to his theme? Here again he is echoing what his readers feel to be true. He (and they) fully believe that a deep division separates our experience of society from those people who only exist in the ethnographic record of explorers, missionaries and anthropologists. And so have sociologists believed ever since.

The belief is created by a couple of quick waves of the hand. First, Weber has taught us to see society in terms of the institutional sectors that we know; these sectors are inhabited by priests, judges, intellectuals, elites, landowners, tenants, and outcasts. In this setting, problems of rationality are posed as problems that only arise in the growth and conflict of these institutions. So peoples whose society does not clearly differentiate judges, priests, landlords, and others, cannot be relevant to modern society. India, China, and Israel are relevant because their history can be presented in terms of the balance or imbalance between these institutional sectors. Australian aborigines and Eskimos just slip between the meshes of the inquiry.

Second, the wand makes another wave. The Hegelian underpinning of Weber's model assumes that the history of the world's institutions records the steady evolution of self-consciousness. Benjamin Nelson (1981) presents a thoughtful and clear account of the Weberian assumptions of evolving human consciousness. So long as it is the end result that we are interested in, then there is little to be gained from examining the early phases of the movement. There is another persuasive idea hidden here, the snobbery of the written word: peoples who have not written down their philosophical meditations cannot have articulated principles for reflection on the social order.

As a contemporary, Durkheim fell into all these institutional traps. He started from the same basic distinction between primitives and moderns and also regarded them as using different mental procedures. It would be stupid to suggest that he did not also subscribe, also with mixed feelings, to the idea of a vanished golden dawn of mankind. The saving grace for him was not to be interested in reconstructing the various phases of evolution that led from the beginning to now. Thus his theory is less heavily loaded with the institutionally given presuppositions. His evolutionary model only has two stages: the primitive stage of mechanical solidarity that is based on shared classifications and the modern stage of organic solidarity based on economic specialization and exchange. If we take away the evolutionary scaffolding from Weber's theory, there is really nothing left except the ranked series of institutions. If we take it away from Durkheim's theory, we are left with two forms of social commitment, one classificatory and one economic. Even Durkheim did not believe that classificatory solidarity was uniquely associated with undeveloped stages of the division of labor, for he devoted much attention to standardized ideas of right and wrong in modern society.

To read *The Elementary Forms of the Religious Life* in isolation from the rest of Durkheim's work is to insure misunderstanding it, for his thinking was a single arch in which each major publication was a necessary statement. He harped always on the one theme, the loss of classificatory solidarity. He deplored its irreplaceability and the crises of individual identity that follow from absence of strong, supporting, publicly shared, and privately internalized classifications. He taught that publicly standardized ideas (collective representations) constitute social order. He recognized that the hold they have upon the individual varies in strength. Calling it moral density, he tried to measure its strength and to assess the effects of its weakness. According to Durkheim, sociological method requires that individual responses be treated as psychological facts to be studied in a frame of reference of individual psychology. Only collective representations are social facts, and social facts count for more than psychological ones because the individual psyche is constituted by the socially constructed classifications. Since the mind is already colonized, we should at least try to examine the colonizing process.

When Durkheim wrote with Marcel Mauss the essay on primitive classification (1903), what had already been a long-term conviction (that true solidarity is based on shared classifications), started to become a method. It is true that Weber related distinctive styles of reasoning to distinctive types of institutions, and therefore, it is true that this is also his program. But his warnings that the sacred had been put to flight and that individuals now stand on unlegitimated territory, and his tribute to the spirit of the age have had a soporific affect. The heavy work of classifying kinds of classification systems and their associated moral attitudes is still barely broached. Yet while everyone else was adopting institutionally prescribed postures about modernity, the loss of legitimacy, wonder and sacredness, Durkheim and Mauss proposed to analyze the extent to which the mundane classifications we use are projections of the social structure partaking in the aura of sacredness. The sacred that Weberians regretted was an unanalyzable mystique. The sacred for Durkheim and Mauss was nothing more mysterious or occult than shared classifications, deeply cherished and violently defended. That is not all: this idea of the sacred is capable of analysis.

In writing about the sacred, Durkheim was trying to put his finger on how institutions do the classifying. His idea was not that sacred power flashes out as an inherent property of constitutions and kings, but the other way around. The peoples he chose to represent the elementary social forms have no constitutions, kings, or any superordinate coercive authority. To the Australians, the sacred can only draw its power from their own consensus. Its coercive strength, which arms the whole universe with punishing taboos to reinforce the individual's wavering commitment, is based on the classifications inside the same individual's head. It is based essentially upon the classifications pertaining to the division of labor. Thus, his theory of the sacred is not just one about disappearing civilizations but also one about moderns, since we also have a society based on the division of labor. The book on suicide (1897) and his development of the idea of anomie are Durkheim's best demonstration that he expected us to learn about ourselves from ethnographic societies.

Durkheim's program of research starts from the possibility that either there is a good fit or a bad fit between the public and the private classifications. If the fit is bad, it can be for two different reasons: the individual may reject the public classifications and refuse to let them have any hold upon his own judgments; or the individual may accept the worth of the public classifications, but know that he or she is incapable of meeting the expected standards. Lastly, the public classifications may be relatively coherent or in a state of incoherence. Following Durkheim, these relations between an individual's state of mind and the standard expectations of his society have been much considered by sociologists as sources of anomie, giving rise to deviant behavior. Indeed, the idea of anomie has a huge literature. Yet deviance has generally not been identified by systematic examination of norms but by signs of rejection by the main society. The deviance that results in change is not counted as anomie. Sociologists have tended to assimilate the complex argument of Durkheim's book on suicide and *The Rules of the Sociological Method* to one distinction, that between insiders and outsiders. The program of research is the relatively simple one of observing the members of a group reclassifying their deviants to the status of outsiders. In *Primitive Classification* the coauthors suggest a very different program. What constitutes deviance cannot be asserted until the dimensions of conformity have been delineated. To assess degrees of conformity among ourselves, we must make the same meticulous count of categories, tracing the way the physical world is turned into a projection of the social world. It is the same for us as for the Eskimos and the Australians; we must use the same method of constructing the north and the south, the right and the left, all loaded with the patterns of dominance, congregation and dispersal, for ourselves as well as for the Chinese and the Zuni Indians.

Admittedly, Durkheim never articulated such a program for modern industrial society. The thought style of his day celebrated social evolution so emphatically that he only saw around him the march of modernization with the inevitable accompaniment of increasing incoherence. He accepted the same popular idea that modern man has escaped from the control of institutions, which was shared by most of his contemporaries. A disciple wishing to defend Durkheim's main thesis against his hesitation to apply it to moderns at least has Durkheim's method as a tool for discovering our own collective representations. The high triumph of institutional thinking is to make the institutions completely invisible. When all the great thinkers of a period agree that the present day is like no other period, and that a great gulf divides us now from our past, we get a first glimpse of a shared classification. Since all social relations can be analyzed as market transactions, the pervasiveness of the market successfully feeds us the conviction that we have escaped from the old non-market institutional controls into a dangerous, new liberty. When we also believe that we are the first generation uncontrolled by the idea of the sacred, and the first to come face to face with one another as real individuals, and that in consequence we are the first to achieve full self-consciousness, there is incontestably a collective representation. Recognizing this, Durkheim would have to concede that primitive solidarity based on shared classification is not completely lost.

To analyze our own collective representations, we should relate what is shared in our mental furnishing to our common experience of authority and work. To know how to resist the classifying pressures of our institutions, we would like to start an independent classificatory exercise. Unfortunately, all the classifications that we have for thinking with are provided ready-made, along with our social life. For thinking about society we have at hand the categories we use as members of society speaking to each other about ourselves. These actor's categories work at every possible level. At the top would be the most general, and at the bottom would be the most particular social rules. When we even try to assign items to this bottom level of least general social classifications, we may catch ourselves thinking of domestic situations and enumerating the roles of children, adults, males, and females. Starting at that point, we automatically reproduce the scheme of authority and the division of labor in the home, but it will be very different if an Indian or an American is thinking as Ravindra Khare, an Indian anthropologist teaching in America has shrewdly observed (Khare 1985, p. 43). Or we may start by taking the roles least involved in social organization, say tramps, and move from the periphery towards the centers of influence. Or we may start with new babies and move up the age structure. In each case, we are adopting the categories used by our administrators for collecting taxes, making population censuses, and estimating the need for schools or prisons. Our minds are running on the old treadmill already. How can we possibly think of ourselves in society except by using the classifications established in our institutions? If we turn to the various social scientists, we find that their minds are still more deeply in thrall. Their professional subject matter is cast in administrative categories, art separated from science, affect from cognition, imagination from reasoning. For purposes of judicial and administrative control, we find persons neatly labeled according to levels of ability, and find thinking classed as rational, insane, criminal, and criminally insane. The work of classifying that is already done for us is performed as a service to instituted professions.

At the same time as institutions produce labels, there is a feedback of Robert Merton's self-fulfilling kind. The labels stabilize the flux of social life and even create to some extent the realities to which they apply. Ian Hacking has taken up the relation between the label and the reality from cues laid by Michel Foucault's study of the "constitution of subjects." This process Hacking calls "making up people" by labeling them and in various ways insuring that they will conform to the labels (1985). Working on nineteenth-century statistics focused on deviation and control of deviants, he suggests that making up people is of recent origin. The anthropologist is immediately inclined to demur. People have always been labeling each other, with the same consequences—labels stick. But Hacking must be right when he adds that "the sheer proliferation of labels during the nineteenth century, may have engendered vastly more kinds of people than ever the world knew before." A veritable avalanche of numbers started to pour out of government statistical offices in Europe from about 1820. The exercise of counting, once started, generated its own thousands of subdivisions. As fast as new medical categories (hitherto unimagined) were invented, or new criminal or sexual or moral categories, new kinds of people spontaneously came forward in hordes to accept the labels and to live accordingly. The responsiveness to new labels suggests extraordinary readiness to fall into new slots and to let selfhood be redefined. This is not like the naming that, according to nominalist philosophers, creates a particular version of the world by picking out certain sorts of things, for instance, naming stars, foregrounding some and letting others disappear from sight. It is a much more dynamic process by which new names are uttered and forthwith new creatures corresponding to them emerge.

Hacking's point is that people are not merely re-labeled and newly made prominent, still behaving as they would behave whether so labeled or not. The new people behave differently than they ever did before.

Elaborating on this difference between people and things: what camels, mountains, and microbes are doing does not depend on our words. What happens to tuberculosis bacilli does depend on whether we poison them with BCG vaccine, but it does not depend upon how we describe them . . . it is the vaccine, not our words, that kills. Human action is more closely linked to human discipline than is bacterial action. (Hacking 1985, p. 13)

Hacking is drawing a distinction between the effect of description on inanimate objects and the effect of names on humans. A course of injections can kill microbes: "possibilities for microbes are delimited by nature, not by words." However, the contrast is not so clear, for it is not the words that do things to the people. The label does not cause them to change their posture and rearrange their bodies. A course of toxic injections could kill people too. Nor are the microbes less responsive to words than humans. For the fair comparison, the labeling process in both cases is part of a larger constraining action, and in both cases the plants and animals and microbes respond even more vehemently than humans. The individual bacillus may die, true enough, but in a very short space of time new breeds have emerged, not to conform to the labels but to defy them, millions of new bacilli appear, never imagined before, but immune to the attacks mounted against them under the old labels. In the same way as sexual perverts, hysterics, or depressive maniacs, living creatures interacting with humans transform themselves to adapt to the new system represented by the labels. The real difference may be that life outside of human society transforms itself away from the labels in self-defense, while that within human society transforms itself towards them in hope of relief or expecting advantage.

The special merit of drawing attention to responsiveness to names is the invitation to philosophers to change their focus. Instead of concentrating on naming as a way of indicating particular items, complete systems of knowledge are unfolded by Foucault's approach. The relation between people and the things they name is never static. As Nelson Goodman says, the relation is within an evolving system (1978). Naming is only one set of inputs; it is on the surface of the classification process. The interaction that Hacking describes goes round, from people making institutions to institutions making classifications, to classifications entailing actions, to actions calling for names, and to people and other living creatures responding to the naming, positively and negatively.

Having accepted that persons classify, we can also recognize that their personal classifying has some degree of autonomy. Communities classify in a different mode. As we have already seen, institutions survive by harnessing all information processes to the task of establishing themselves. The instituted community blocks personal curiosity, organizes public memory, and heroically imposes certainty on uncertainty. In marking its own boundaries it affects all lower level thinking, so that persons realize their own identities and classify each other through community affiliation. Since it uses the division of labor as a source of metaphors to affirm itself, the community's self-knowledge and knowledge of the world must undergo change when the organization of work changes. When it reaches a new level of economic activity new forms of classification must be designed. But individual persons do not control the classifying. It is a cognitive process that involves them in the same way as they are involved in the strategies and payoffs of the economic scene or in the constitution of language. Individual persons make choices within the classifications. Something else governs their choices, some need of easier communication, a call for a new focus for precision. The change will be a response to the vision of a new kind of community.

For example, why have wines suddenly changed their labels? The customers of the Cheese Cellar in Evanston now select their wine by the varietal name of the grape. Is this anyone's real choice? Did any one restaurateur take the decision no more to offer for sale Bordeaux, Burgundy, Loire, or Rhine wines, St. Emilion or Sauterne? What does it mean for the theory of classification that customers now are asking for Zinfandel, Gamay, or Sauvignon, even though the wine may hail from Bordeaux?

The same mode has renamed textiles. They used to come classed by place names, shantung and crepe de chine from China, paisley from Paisley, poplin from Avignon, cambric from Cambrai, lisle from Lille, cashmere from Cashmere, Macclesfield silk from Macclesfield. Now they are labeled pure cotton, pure silk, pure wool, nylon, polyester, or rayon. Gold and silver hallmarks are based on place of origin, but now sheer weight often tells more. Children's zoology books still classify birds and animals by regions. Encyclopedias of mythology present myths as coming from Greece, Rome, the Celtic fringe, or India. Global statistics, a sophisticated interpretive exercise which is still in its infancy, uses the world atlas approach. In the Bible the label Judean, Nazarene, or Samarian said a lot about the person. But now the classifications by genetic makeup, educational, psychiatric, or occupational status make a difference. Lawrence Rosen has expressed the contrast clearly in the idea of the person as an identity negotiated within a community. Social identity in Morocco starts with the idea of place, not merely place of origin, but also the whole sum of spatially bounded negotiations and networks which a person has achieved.

> A very considerable part of an individual's character is constituted by the social milieu from which he draws his nurture. To Moroccans, geographical regions are inhabited spaces, realms within which communities organize themselves to wrest a living and forge a degree of security . . . their main focus is on the identity of persons *in situ* because the site itself is a social context through which an individual becomes used to ways of creating a lived in space. To be attached to a place is, therefore, not only to have a point of origin—it is to have those social roots, those human achievements, that are distinctive to the kind of person one is. (1984, p. 23)

Elsewhere, Rosen contrasts this view of a person as having roots in a group and a place with a modern view.

> Thus where an American may wish first to place another by asking what he *does* (i.e., what occupation he practices) because such information conveys a host of implications for economic, social and political attitudes, in Morocco, the central question is "where are your origins," since it is this information which, initially, conveys a degree of predictability about the sort of ties that are possible with such a man.

Something happens to the insides of our heads when a different kind of organization had made obsolete the old classifications by places. The change is not a deliberate or conscious choice. Institutions veil their influence, so that we hardly notice any change.

One of these shifts in thought is recorded in the fate of Savary des Bruslon's *Dictionnaire Universel du Commerce*. Savary was a royal customs official in the reign of Louis XIV. His dictionary of commerce was a first attempt to systematize the knowledge held by merchants, producers, government officials, and consumers. From it William Reddy tries to glean "the mental landscape of the textile trade at the beginning of the eighteenth century" (Reddy 1986). "First issued between 1723 and 1730 and reissued, pirated, and translated at least six more times between 1741 and 1784," it had an extraordinary initial success. But by 1784 the new edition was hardly more than an inconsistent patchwork of revisions. So much had happened in 43 years that a completely new dictionary was needed, organized according to a new rational scheme, corresponding to the changes in commerce and manufacture. But on the eve of the revolution, such rethinking was impossible.

For writing such classificatory documents as guidebooks and dictionaries, the institutions that are in place do the classifying themselves. To describe the ins and outs of the eighteenth-century textile trade, Savary had needed the skills of a connoisseur. Everyone engaged in the trade was exercising a complex, community-focused connoisseurship, based on the names of places, the names of guilds, and the seals by which their products could be recognized and quality guaranteed.

Various attempts after the revolution to edit and update a dictionary failed until 1837, when Guillaumin Publishers produced a new one altogether, written by a large committee of professors, merchants, and bankers. After 50 years experience of free trade, regulation is no longer an issue; "nothing stands between the producer and the purchaser; the production process itself is therefore the only possible source of distinctions for determining what a cloth is." By this time the guilds are gone. The results which they guaranteed and which were Savary's main concern have been replaced in the dictionary by processes and materials and costs, organized alphabetically. New categories have been named, and pages and pages are devoted to the raw materials, to the plants, their places of origin, and to the fiber—its chemical and mechanical properties and the stages of its transformation into thread. Some categories of cloth have broadened; there is less to say about specific varieties of cloth; production is the main preoccupation.

Reddy describes the 1837 dictionary as an immense task of rethinking. The very notion of a commodity had changed and every specific commodity used in Europe had to be reconceived. As Reddy analyzes the different categories in the two dictionaries, he lays bare a particular kind of change in the economy. The making of cloth has been disengaged from the institutions of the old regime. It is no longer responding to the tastes in dress of a stratified society, nor to the regulations and privileges of a corps of urban weavers and merchants, nor to the customs of peasant producers working in the hinterland, nor to the methods of operation of the government in Versailles. The institutions of the textile industry have reached a level of organization at which a dictionary can list their processes and materials independently as those of a manufacturing sector of a market economy.

So what about the French wine trade? It is the California wine industry, following similar processes of industrialization, that has so forced the change of nomenclature that the atlas approach to the classification of wine, which worked well for Europe, is no longer appropriate. These two diagrams show the difference. Six of the most renowned producers of Bordeaux and six of the most ambitious wine producers in the Napa Valley have been chosen to match each other, not only in the quality of their wines but also in scale. On the French side, the range of production is from 3,750 to 30,000 cases per year. Some Californian wineries produce upwards of 1,000,000 cases per year, but it is not difficult to match the French scale of production. This establishes that scale is not a decisive difference in the shift to be described.

The Californian production is highly differentiated. Each winery produces a large variety of wines, each from a different grape, while the French producers tend to specialize in one or two wines and one blend of grapes.

In the French classification the geographical factor is prominent. One can start by saying that Bordeaux is a region in France; within Bordeaux are the smaller regions, Médoc, St. Emilion, Graves, Côtes; the concentric circles focus down onto the chateaux. Then a quality principle enters. Médoc has a classification based on the average price fetched by the wine over the 100 years preceding 1855. Undoubtedly, this classification identified the best land for vineyards. The classification by quality recognizes first, second, third, and fourth growths, and at the bottom of the scale a *Cru Bourgeois*. Below this level are unclassed growths. On this criterion of quality the chateau is not considered as a plot of land so much as a brand name of whose reputation the owner is extremely

Figure 1
SIX WINE PRODUCERS IN THE BORDEAUX REGION

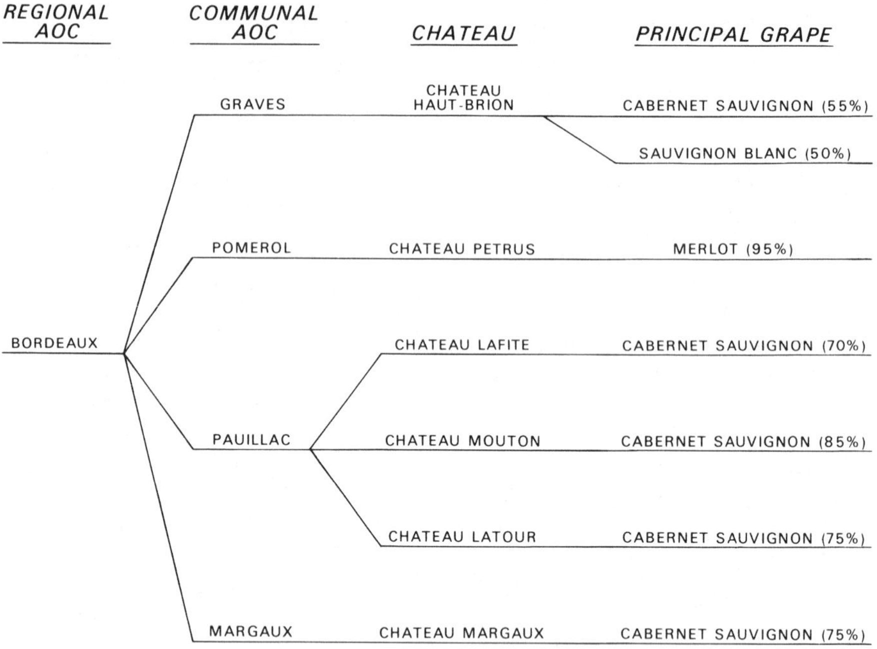

REGIONAL AOC	COMMUNAL AOC	CHATEAU	PRINCIPAL GRAPE
	GRAVES	CHATEAU HAUT-BRION	CABERNET SAUVIGNON (55%)
			SAUVIGNON BLANC (50%)
	POMEROL	CHATEAU PETRUS	MERLOT (95%)
BORDEAUX		CHATEAU LAFITE	CABERNET SAUVIGNON (70%)
	PAUILLAC	CHATEAU MOUTON	CABERNET SAUVIGNON (85%)
		CHATEAU LATOUR	CABERNET SAUVIGNON (75%)
	MARGAUX	CHATEAU MARGAUX	CABERNET SAUVIGNON (75%)

careful. Since the Médoc owners have inherited their rank position from the 1855 classification of quality, they are subject to self-imposed standards. In St. Emilion the quality is checked by a committee; some of the most famous chateaux, the *Premiers Grands Crus,* have to renew their right to their high place in the classification every ten years. Others, the *Grands Crus,* have to submit each vintage for tasting. In either case, the great concern to maintain quality and to maintain a name is like the concern of the cloth guilds to do the same. And like the guilds, each chateau makes its own special product. Naming the wine after the region and the chateau is to condense information that can only be unpacked by connoisseurship. The name encapsulates a tried process, a traditional blend of grapes, a soil, the slope of a valley, and a climate. It defies any other rationalization. And, like the cloth guilds, it is a monopolistic institution to protect the producer. It belongs to a system of customs and excise control. The chateau and

Figure 2
SIX WINE PRODUCERS IN THE NAPA VALLEY

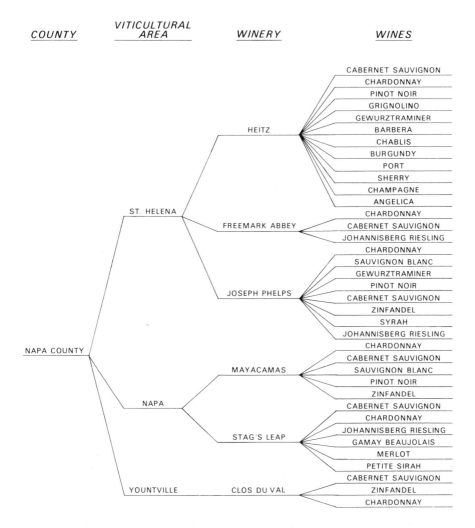

COUNTY	VITICULTURAL AREA	WINERY	WINES

regional names could not be attached to wines in California without violating a property right.

This was one reason why Californian wines could only call themselves Bordeaux-type or Burgundy-type. But they were not tempted to try to establish a Napa Valley type. They surely might have been able to do that, if Californian wine had been developed in an earlier period before large-scale marketing for a whole continent was within their scope. Now who can say whether, like Bordeaux wines, their product might have been able to concentrate upon an unmistakable, standardized yet varied, Napa identity? Instead they chose or were driven along the path of diversification. Their classification is based upon the kind of grape. Two wineries on our diagram each use three kinds of grape for three kinds of wine. One uses twelve. The branching out of varietal types in the Californian wine industry writes in large the specialization within a winery. If we were to follow out methods of viticulture, or treatment of the wine at various stages, or techniques of bottling or corking, the same fanning out of experimental processes and production of specialized types of wine would be shown. What Weber called a pragmatic, means-ends, market-oriented type of rationality has emerged. Each winery is seeking a diverse range of specialized wines within a highly diversified market. *The World Atlas of Wines* (Johnson 1981), which uses place so well for explaining French wines, is as irrelevant to the Californian scene as Savary's dictionary of commerce was for describing French textiles in the nineteenth century postrevolutionary structure, and for the same reasons. Large-scale industrial processes are their own institutions. They cannot be embedded in the patterns of local, community control.

This is how the names get changed and how the people and things are rejigged to fit the new categories. First the people are tempted out of their niches by new possibilities of exercising or evading control. Then they make new kinds of institutions, and the institutions make new labels, and the label makes new kinds of people. The next step in understanding how we understand ourselves would be to classify kinds of institutions and the kinds of classification they typically use. There is likely to be a distinctive type of classificatory process that belongs to religious institutions and other distinctive types belonging to medical, pedagogic, military and other institutions. The dictionaries of the French textile industry show that classifications emanating from administrative institutions have a territorial base while those emanating from manufacturing institutions focus on production. What the classifications are devised for and what they can and cannot do are different in each case. A classification of classificatory styles would be a good first step towards thinking systematically about distinctive styles of reasoning. It would be a challenge to the sovereignty of our own institutionalized thought style. The comparison of classifications as an index of other things that are happening in our own society provides a small, provisional ladder of escape from the circle of self-reference. We can look at our own classifications just as well as we can look at our own skin and blood under a microscope. We can recognize regularities appearing in whole arrays of classificatory work, just as well as grammarians can study regularities in syntax and phonetic shifts. There is nothing self-contradictory or absurd in taking a systematic look at the classifications we make of ourselves. The logical difficulties start when we try to develop value-free ideas about the good society. And yet these difficulties must be met if we are not to leave the whole inquiry in a stew of philosophical relativism. It is not at all the purpose of this book to teach that because institutions do so much of our thinking there can be no comparisons between different versions of the world, still less to teach that all versions are equally right or wrong.

9

Institutions Make Life and Death Decisions

A COMFORTING but false idea about institutional thinking has gained some recent currency. This is the notion that institutions just do the routine, low-level, day-to-day thinking. Andrew Schotter, who has so well described institutions as machines for thinking, believes that the minor decisions get off-loaded for institutional processing, while the mind of the individual is left free to weigh important and difficult matters (Schotter 1981 p. 149). There is no reason to believe in any such benign dispensation. The contrary is more likely to prevail. The individual tends to leave the important decisions to his institutions while busying himself with tactics and details. To demonstrate this it is best to restate the initial question.

We have insisted above that it is highly improbable that institutions could emerge smoothly from a gathering momentum of converging interests and an unspecified mixture of coercion and convention. We have too much experience of how easily they come apart and collapse. The thing to be explained is how institutions ever start to stabilize. To become stable means settling into some recognizable shape. It is amazing how institutions fall into stable types that we can recognize in different times and circumstances. The fact that we can talk of a bureaucracy of Byzantine complexity, or that we can recognize monetary instruments in exotic forms is evidence of enduring types of institutions. Institutional economics suggests why a particular institutional form makes more sense to

111

rational individuals in one economic environment rather than another. It does not explain the process by which the institution keeps itself and the environment stable enough to be recognized by the individual making a rational choice.

Information theory draws our attention particularly to divergent patterns. It assumes that for any given pattern a prior buildup of energy is needed. A pattern of given complexity, once stabilized, uses less energy than was required to bring it into existence. For example, heat under a pan of water takes time before the water begins to swirl and bubble. If more energy is pumped in, it has to be used up by new patterns of complexity. So if the heat under the pan is increased, the water will swirl around in a more and more complex pattern. There has to be some way of dissipating any energy that is in excess of what is necessary to maintain the pattern (Prigogine 1980). Over and above a certain point, the extra input of energy will not be able to be absorbed by increasing complexity, and there will be a radical change in the whole pattern. For example, the water will turn into steam. To write of institutions as complex patterns of information (as Schotter does), and to think of the relative efficiency of their channels of communication (as O. E. Williamson does), should lead to considering the amount of energy used for making a particular kind of institution and how it is deployed in a more complex or less complex pattern. And from here it should lead to assessing the volume of transactions that it is capable of handling. Otherwise, information theory in political science is mere academic window dressing, a new favorite metaphor to replace the outdated functionalist metaphor of the 1950s.

Any institution that is going to keep its shape needs to gain legitimacy by distinctive grounding in nature and in reason: then it affords to its members a set of analogies with which to explore the world and with which to justify the naturalness and reasonableness of the instituted rules, and it can keep its identifiable continuing form.

Any institution then starts to control the memory of its members; it causes them to forget experiences incompatible with its righteous image, and it brings to their minds events which sustain the view of nature that is complementary to itself. It provides the categories of their thought, sets the terms for self-knowledge, and fixes identities. All of this is not enough. It must secure the social edifice by sacralizing the principles of justice.

This is Durkheim's doctrine of the sacred. All the other controls exerted by institutions are invisible, but not the sacred. According to Durkheim, the sacred is to be recognized by these three characteristics. First, it is dangerous. If the sacred is profaned, terrible things will happen; the world will break up and the profaner will be crushed. Second, any attack on the sacred rouses emotions to its defense. Third, it is invoked explicitly. There are sacred words and names, sacred places, books, flags, and totems. Such symbols make the sacred tangible, but they in no way limit its range. Entrenched in nature, the sacred flashes out from salient points to defend all the classifications and theories that uphold the institutions. For Durkheim, the sacred is essentially an artifact of society. It is a necessary set of conventions resting on a particular division of labor which, of course produces the needful energy for that kind of system (Durkheim 1893). The sacred makes a fulcrum on which nature and society come into equilibrium, each reflecting the other and each sustaining the known.

No one has much problem with this idea of the sacred. They think of Australian totems and sacred emblems of medieval kings. But, inconsistently, David Hume's teaching that justice is an artificial virtue gives a lot of trouble. The idea that justice is a necessary social construct is exactly parallel to Durkheim's idea of the sacred, but Hume clearly refers to us, ourselves. He brings our idea of the sacred under scrutiny. Our defensive reaction against Hume is exactly what Durkheim would predict. We cannot allow our precepts of justice to depend on artifice. Such teaching is immoral, a threat to our social system with all its values and classifications. Justice is the point that seals legitimacy.

For this very reason, it is difficult to think about it impartially. In spite of a wide belief in the modern loss of mystery, the idea of justice still remains to this day obstinately mystified and recalcitrant to analysis. If we are ever to think against the pressure of our institutions, this is the hardest place to try, where the resistance is strongest. On this subject anthropologists have a privileged position for they record many diverse social forms each venerating its particular idea of justice.

Hume's idea of the artificial virtues is integral to his skeptical program (1739, 1751). It was part of his attack on all theories of innate ideas, whether of causality, natural law, or private property. His radical constructivism makes him exactly the anthropologists' philosopher. When it is a matter of finding logical structures in nature, Hume says that all we ever see there are frequencies, and from these we form habits and expectations. When it is a matter of natural justice, all we can ever know is that we need regulated interactions; to meet the need we develop principles. Accordingly, the idea of justice is not a natural response as to an emotion or to an appetite. As an intellectual system, it has a kind of second-order naturalness because it is a necessary condition for human society. Fabricated precisely for the purpose of justifying and stabilizing institutions, it is founded on conventions in exactly the sense quoted above from David Lewis (1969). Thus, no single element of justice has innate rightness: for being right it depends upon its generality, its schematic coherence, and its fit with other accepted general principles. Justice is a more or less satisfactory intellectual system designed to secure the coordination of a particular set of institutions.

If this turns out to be logically unassailable and yet unacceptable to philosophers who are otherwise strong on logic we shall chalk it up as another instance of the power of the sacred to rouse an emotional defense. For example, the Victorian philosopher who devotedly edited Hume's *Inquiry* and *Treatise* rejected his idea of justice out of hand, treating it as an aberration, the teasing trick of an *enfant terrible*. L. A. Selby-Bigge found Hume's argument about justice to be awkward, ungainly, unintelligible, and unnecessary: "It is pretty plain that he meant it to be offensive" (Selby-Bigge 1893 p. XXVIII).

Hume's approach does not allow us to refuse the name of justice to a system merely because it does not accord with our own. Philosophers can hardly dismiss all civilizations antecedent to our own as defective in moral judgment without seeming to be biased. In other contexts they do not allow one another to appeal to intuition or to an ineffable sense of rightness. When Hercules Poirot caught the Countess Rossakoff with stolen jewels, she denied any intuitive rightness of private property: "And what I feel is, why not? Why should one person own a thing more than another?" (Christie 1935). The trouble with trying to defend an immutable principle of justice is that not everyone sees the self-evident thing. Rules that now seem to us moderns as monstrously unjust did not strike our forebears as wrong. Slavery and the subjugation of women are vulnerable to the same arguments that Hume used against the intuitive right to property.

Ownership is no longer the prominent political issue in our

day. Our own institutions have entrenched equality as the overriding priority. How should it be otherwise in a society that has dispersed private property rights among shareholders and insurance companies and is moving to a vertical organization of professions? The vertical segments need to recruit and promote talent: equality of opportunity is their necessary condition (Perkin 1969). The institutions require that equality of access be incorporated into the central, legitimizing principles. They use lack of equality as blame for delegitimizing rival regimes. They count abhorrent societies that are stratified by horizontal layers peaking to a central pyramid top. Yet this is another mode of organizing, using another energy and communications base, with its own appropriate legitimizing principles.

   Whenever the Western nations colonize an ancient civilization, this conflict between ideas of justice brings tension. In Bali the Dutch colonists found two systems of justice already in place: at the local village level, equality was supported by the old Balinese system; at other levels, the law codes expressed the influence of a hierarchical Hindu system. The former was acceptable to the Dutch administrators, the latter was horrific. In the legal codes, someone who:

> committed an offense against another of a higher caste produced aggravating circumstances, while in the opposite case extenuating circumstances were assumed. A Sudra who seriously offended a Brahmana was condemned to death; a Brahmana who offended a Sudra was merely required to pay a fine worth a few dimes. If an inferior does bodily harm to a superior, there results a punishment by mutilation, such as cutting off hands or feet. (Boon 1977, p. 49, quoting the 1917 *Encyclopedia of the Dutch East Indies*)

James Boon remarks that these harsh and prejudicial punishments dismayed Western observers and also that

> reading between the lines of post-1849 reports, it is obvious that no simple explanation of blind oppression could explain commoner support of such differences. The lower strata actually seem to believe their betters merited milder penalties for ostensibly the same offense. Dutch administrators in Bali might have been able to accept radical hierarchy in title, learn-

ing, residence, property, religious merit, and so forth. But never in legal, specially criminal proceedings. In the conflict of two legal systems we can best sense the poignance of that storied meeting, and mutual failure to comprehend, between the Ancient East and the New West. (p. 49)

Given that equality as a natural right or as a universal principle of justice is still the most prominent difference between Western and many other systems of justice, it is not enough simply to dismiss all of the latter as obviously unjust. And yet there are many distinguished philosophers who do just that.

Consider Alan Gewirth's attempt to establish a supreme principle of morality on which all other moral principles depend and to use it to prove that inequality is unjust. The argument of *Reason and Morality* (1978) is scholarly, impressive, and truly seductive. Its strategy is to unpack what is logically entailed in the concept of a rational agent. Agents want to achieve their goals; therefore, they want freedom to act and the well-being for acting. The wants are intrinsic to the concept of agency: therefore, agents' wants turn into claims. Recognizing that his own claims are valid against all other agents, the rational agent must, for consistency's sake, acknowledge that the same claims by other agents are valid against himself. Not to recognize what is implied in rational agency is to act against reason. From this logical basis, Gewirth's scheme extends to substantive moral principles, including the necessary equality of agents.

Taking as its premise the wishes of a rational agent, Gewirth has formulated an argument based on logically derived wants and on fittingness similar to the one used by the twelfth century theologians. To clinch the question of whether the Virgin Mary was born without originals sin they proposed first that God would have wanted her to be immaculately conceived, as something built into the idea of God; second, they drew in the argument that God is omnipotent and so it follows that it would have been perfectly possible for him to do what he wanted. This led to the triumphant conclusion that he did do it. One form emphasizes his wish: *potuit, voluit, fecit.* Another emphasizes the fittingness implicit in the logical scheme: *potuit, decuit, ergo fecit.* It has been said that Alan Gewirth is impervious to standard objections to the ontological argument for the existence of God (Nielsen 1984). Both he and the scholastics have an argument that depends on unpacking the logical implications of certain words—what else can logic ever do? But we have said enough in earlier chapters to show that the package of ideas that makes up the meaning of a word is itself the product of institutional thinking.

From his "Principle of Generic Consistency" Gewirth expects to make not only the rightness of equality, but also the wrongness of murder and slavery emerge (1978). But what comes under the heading of murder? He answers that murder refers to the killing of innocent humans that has as its reason or nature only gain or gratification of desire. But what comes under the heading of innocence? If the other categories of thought are culturally defined, are guilt, innocence, oppression, and coercion allowed to be exceptions? As Lena Jayyusi points out, the categories of law are embedded in a normative and moral framework, tied to responsibilities, and embedded in the everyday practical order (Jayyusi 1984, p. 4). She goes on to argue, for instance, that to decontextualize the concepts of coercion and oppression as developed in the West and apply them to Soviet institutions, is logically misplaced. The use of the word "coercion" presupposes the relevance of rights whose infringement motivates the description. If a social and political system denies rights to private capital accumulation, then for a subject to be deprived of that to which no prior right exists is not oppressive or coercive in the same sense as it would be elsewhere. The program Jayyusi advocates will study conversational practice and relevance rules. What a pity that it depends heavily on speech and does not include power structures and patterns of interaction. Without that dimension the moral construction put on the verbal concepts cannot be traced to another source of evidence, and so their interpretation cannot be independently validated. She is only taking a preliminary step toward the classification of category systems. The full exercise would classify the social order at the same time.

Without appeal to religion, intuitionism, or innate ideas, it is very hard to defend a substantive principle of justice as universally right. Brian Barry is another well-known philosopher who wishes to defend the principle of equality and so takes issue with Hume's concept of justice as an artificial virtue. According to Hume's theory, the need for a concept of justice would only arise in certain circumstances. It would never emerge in conditions of perfect ease and affluence, for there would be no need for a universal regulative principle. It would never emerge when one party had overwhelm-

ing might, for the powerful are not disposed to let general principles affect their self-interested action. For Hume, abstract, formal
standards of justice are only worked out between proximate
equals. Barry finds that he can meaningfully apply such standards
to unequal relations, and that their applicability shows that justice
rests on principle not on convention.

> When we take standards of justice that would be agreed upon
> by a group of equals and apply them to condemn a society
> pervaded by systematic group discrimination, we are in a
> sense making use of independent and external criteria. (Barry
> 1978, p. 225)

To Barry, it seems a decisive point against Hume if we can discuss
ruthless exploitation in terms of justice. The fact that we can apply
the concept of injustice shows, in his view, that the idea of justice is
universal and independent of local circumstances. Someone may,
for example, freely consent to an unjust arrangement because he
incorrectly believes it to be required by justice.

> Suppose in some society it were universally accepted that
> some people were by birth entitled to economic and social
> privilege. There would be no conflict over distribution, yet we
> would surely say that this social system was unjust. (Barry
> 1978, p. 219)

In these opinions, Barry is expressing the legitimating principles of the conventions created to maintain a particular set of
institutions, to wit, those of Western industrial society. Yes, for us,
who have internalized the justice of these institutions, such inequality is clearly unjust. The more the discrimination by birth
and the larger the gap between the entitlements of different
classes, the more we would condemn the inequality of it. Yet,
however vehemently we assert our own principles of justice, they
are still the principles that have emerged over the last two hundred
years, along with the emergence of an economic system based on
individual contract. Turning itself from a horizontal pattern of
integration to a vertical one, which depends on drawing independent individuals up from bottom to top, the whole information
system has to be transformed. When the perturbation has reached

a certain point, the dissipative structures can no longer hold the pattern. First, the founding analogies need revision. Louis Dumont has traced the eighteenth-century effort to refocus its ideology away from organic metaphors. He shows that Mandeville's parable of the independent industrious individual bees was a landmark in the turning away of Western thought from hierarchical models of society toward justifying individualism (Dumont 1977, pp. 83–104).

When the analogy with nature has been changed, the system of justice also needs revision. Now it has to promote the vertical movement of individuals instead of containing them within their horizontal layers. The result has been the sacralization of a society based on an extravagant use of energy unprecedent in the history of the world. This is a society that uses equality of individuals to justify itself, but in world-wide comparisons of justice its economic ascendancy and its efforts to maintain its unequal advantage become hard to justify by its own principles of legitimation. We can join Barry in feeling outrage, pity, and shame at the exploitation of the weak. Our humane feelings do nothing to dislodge Hume's argument.

According to Hume, the artificial virtues are to be known by their internal coherence within an abstract system that harmonizes everyday interactions in a particular society. Brian Barry is defending an absolute idea of justice. Where can it be founded if not in intuition? He says:

> If someone can read a history of European settlements in Australia and the Americas, or a history of negro slavery, without admitting that he is reading about a history of monstrous injustice, I doubt if anything that I can say is likely to convince him. (Barry 1978, p. 22)

In other words, this feeling is ultimately incommunicable. If Gewirth used the ontological argument on behalf of equality, Barry in the same cause has adopted something very like Rudolph Otto's justification of religious truth: if the reader has never had a mystic experience, if he has never felt the Mysterium Tremendum, if he is stranger to the sense of the numinous, then, says Otto the Lutheran theologian, nothing I can say will convince him: the feeling is incommunicable. Hume's answer to Countess Rossakoff, as well as to philosophers with contrary intuitions, would be to recall that the functioning of a society depends on some degree of coherence and that an abstract summary of the interlocking principles on which it works promotes coordination. Once formulated the artifice acquires venerability. Durkheim could explain why, like an ivy-covered wall for a new university, justice seems to have been there forever. It had to have existed long before humans came into the world; so it appears old and immutable as one of nature's fixtures, above challenge.

At this point the question about moral relativism becomes pressing. Has the argument cut the ground from under itself? Put crudely, the case is that moral opinions are prepared by the social institutions. It is very rare and difficult for an individual to choose a moral stand on individual rational grounds. In that case, our own judgments are likewise prepared in our own social institutions. So the charge is that we have no way of comparing their value: all we can do is describe; we can never say that justice requires equality or defend private property or rebuke enslavement; we have reduced all moral judgements to expressions of different societies.

Several issues seem to be mixed up. The worst of all is the charge of falling into contradiction and absurdity. The next worst is the idea that total tolerance of any kind of behavior would follow logically. The least damaging is the idea that because we have said that moral ideas are an essential part of the social institutions they can neither be compared nor judged, but this is also untrue.

On Hume's principles we can say that one system is more just than another. We can say it on two counts, one logical and one practical. According to his teaching, a system of justice is devised expressly for providing coherent principles on which social behavior can be organized. So we can compare systems of justice in respect of their coherence. This is the regular task of historical jurisprudence. Judicial reform is often justified on grounds of incoherence among the principles being used. According to Hume, arbitrariness defeats the essential purpose of justice. We can compare the amount of arbitrary rules. So there is no problem on this issue. On the practical count, we can start by asking how well a system of justice actually performs the task of providing abstract principles for regulating behavior. It could be too arcane, too complex, and too ramifying to be understood. By simple tests we can decide whether the system of justice of one country, say of a colonial power, relates precisely enough to the context of another place, say Africa. For example, did the old Tudor law relating to the practice of witchcraft in England help district officers to deal with witchcraft accusations in the Sudan? Do Western laws against bigamy work well to regulate affairs between Moslem polygamists in London? Or, on another kind of practical test, is the system of justice efficient? Are the courts too remote from the centers of population? Jurists make these and other comparisons of systems of justice all the time. In doing so they are not obliged to apply the validating principles of their own institutions, not at all. The tests of coherence and non-arbitrariness, complexity and practicality, are not subjective preferences. It is as straightforward to study human systems of justice objectively as it is to measure the length of human feet from heel to toe. Systems can be compared as systems. The one thing that it is not possible to do is to pick a particular virtue, say kindness to animals or to the aged, or equality, and find a way of proving that it is always and ineluctably right and best.

Finally, recognizing the social origin of ideas of justice does not commit us to refraining from judging between systems. They can be judged better or worse according to the good sense we can make of their assumptions. Suppose a system of justice assumed that only a third of the population submitted to its rulings were fully human. We could be objective in our reasons for thinking that the other two thirds were human beings. At this point the question of moral relativism has merged into questions about what is real and what illusionary in the world. I hope there is no need to get into the argument about realism. What has been said above does not throw into doubt that there are objective tests of right and wrong versions of the world and how it works. For example, imagine a system of justice that punished people for what they are alleged to have done in other people's dreams. It would not be difficult to show that such a system draws the lines of responsibility according to a wrong version of reality and a wrong version of human accountability—so much so that it could not be organized coherently on any practical issue. The way that humans are, the facts that they walk upright and cannot be in two places at once, are incorporated as part of any system of justice. Some experience and study of the conditions of life have gone into the background of the thinking. All that is being argued here and throughout this book is that this cumulative experience of the world should explicitly incorporate the social nature of cognition and judgment.

The preferred assumption, which implies that humans are not essentially social beings, is strong enough to prevent us seeing how they actually behave. What happens when law is abrogated? Does nature take over? We have been saying that nature is culturally defined, that individual minds are furnished with culturally given attitudes. So what happens? Hume himself supposed that in a famine each would seize what he needed to survive, throwing concepts of private property to the winds. Part of his demonstration of their artificiality was to show that criteria of justice would be suspended when it is a matter of starvation. Other philosophers agree. But starving people do not rise up and seize the food that is there. Sheer force is not all that stops them from looting the stores. Within the family or village in such a crisis who starves and dies or who eats and lives is neither quite random nor dependent on force. Strongest and most numerous do not always take all when the tragic crisis arrives. History shows that famine does not automatically revoke conventions. It does not usher in something like a natural law of equal rights. By adopting such an assumption we naturalize our own ideas of equity; it is as if we assume that when nature takes over, she does what we knew we ought to have done all along, that is, to distribute equally. Crisis behavior depends on what patterns of justice have been internalized, what institutions have been legitimated.

A conflict has sometimes been reported between international relief agencies and local officials. The international agents from the industrial West try to distribute food supplies with an even hand. Equality of rights to survival is the unquestioned principle. With dismay they find that they cannot recruit representatives of local institutions to help in their work. To give out the food as quickly as possible, existing channels of distribution would be the most efficient and most acceptable to the famine-stricken country. But no! As soon as the local people are brought into the relief scheme, the food gets diverted. The poorest are always the most vulnerable in a famine. But the food does not reach them. Hoarding, stealing, exploiting, recrimination, and self-righteous indignation are part of the grim story of famine relief.

William Torry is an anthropologist who has been studying responses to famine (Torry 1984). He has observed famine in the context of the isolated village or province where no foreign relief is available. This experience has led him to question whether the dire crisis is producing a breakdown of norms. Instead, he finds a community switching from its regular set of moral principles to its regular emergency set. The emergency system is not an abrogation of all principles. Torry does not see a collapse of conventions. On the contrary, the emergency system starts with a gradual tightening and narrowing of the normal distributive principles. It is foreseen that there will not be enough food for everybody. The emergency system starts to give short rations to the disadvantaged, the marginal, the politically ineffectual. Protecting those in command and those already advantaged results in the skeletal institutions being preserved and the usual channels of communication being kept open. The effect is to maintain some minimal level of operations. As the crisis deepens and as he watches, he witnesses with horror a systematic destruction of certain categories of persons. He can recognize who is predestined to starve—and so can the victims. He traces the lines of victimage through the selection processes of the regular social system. Whatever are the normative principles of exclusion from privilege or security—whether by birth, or office, or sex, or age, or by definition of deviancy and criminality—these regular exclusions point to who will get less as resources diminish and who will finally be turned out or left behind to starve. To his surprise, the preordained victims meekly accept their fate. When the famine is over, some of them may have survived, but they will surely have lost children and kin. Torry watches to see how community life is resumed. Given the coldblooded inequity of what has happened, he wonders if the survivors will show resentment against their exploiters. They do not. They recognize the doom of their families as fitting and as a normal part of crisis conditions. They understand that the elite were never in danger. They take up their old relationships of service gratefully, without grievance. Their acceptance of their victimage indicates to Torry that he has witnessed not a destruction of the social order, but its affirmation.

Is this a sinister story? Torry wonders whether the crisis morality has made the wreckage less or more than it would have been otherwise. That it seems to make recovery quicker expresses a favorite dilemma for moral philosophers. Should we look to the consequences of our choices, or should we do what is ineluctably right? If all on the lifeboat will eventually die if water is distributed evenly, and if there is a good chance that some will be saved if distribution is restricted, what should be done? And if selection is right, who should be saved? The hereditary elite? The cleverest? The hardiest? The weakest?

This is the problem that confronted the party of explorers imprisoned in the cave without food. It is a sort of problem that is insoluble if it is given to individuals as an intellectual puzzle. First, the case is isolated from all institutional context. Justice has nothing to do with isolated cases. Second, individuals normally off-load such decisions on to institutions. No private ratiocination can find the answer. The most profound decisions about justice are not made by individuals as such, but by individuals thinking within and on behalf of institutions. The only way that a system of justice exists is by its everyday fulfillment of institutional needs. If this be conceded, it would appear that the rational-choice philosophers fail to focus on the point at which rational choice is exercised. Choosing rationally, on this argument, is not choosing intermittently among crises or private preferences, but choosing continuously among social institutions. It follows that moral philosophy is an impossible enterprise if it does not start with the constraints on institutional thinking. So let no one take comfort in the thought that primitives think through their institutions while moderns take the big decisions individually. That very thought is an example of letting institutions do the thinking.

In rich Western industrial society, a new medical advance can create the same dilemma as the famine or the lifeboat. There is now a significant literature on the response of different countries to the policy choice raised in the early history of kidney dialysis. The Seattle Artificial Kidney Center used the following principles:

> A person "worthy" of having his life preserved by a scarce expensive treatment like chronic dialysis was one judged to have qualities such as decency and responsibility. Any history of social deviance, such as a prison record, any suggestion that a person's married life was not intact and scandal-free, were strong counter indications to selection.
>
> The preferred candidate was a person who had demonstrated achievement through hard work and success at his job, who went to church, joined groups, and was actively involved in community affairs. (Fox and Swarez 1974; p. 247)

Supposing there were too many persons about to die for lack of the treatment, so that need could not be a discriminating criterion. What will be a better policy? There are two big differences between this situation in modern industrial Seattle and the small, famine-stricken communities struggling with what is formally the same problem. First, the Seattle Committee was secret. Perhaps for that reason it earned the comment of a psychiatrist and a lawyer that

> Justice requires a fairer method than the unbridled consciences, the built-in biases, and the fantasies of a secret committee. (Barry, 1978, pp. 212–13)

Second, kidney dialysis was a brand new invention. So there were no existing institutions to set the priorities. Presumably, in the case of the famine community falling back on its emergency justice, everybody has internalized the rules. Something very like the decision of the Seattle Committee would probably be applied unquestionably if the President of the United States had fallen victim to kidney disease. He would be rushed ahead of the line, and no one would protest. The Seattle conscience seems fantastic and unbridled because no one accepts its judgments of success and scandal as legitimate. What would have been really fantastic? Perhaps to reserve the treatment only to save the lives of convicts serving life sentences, so that justice would not be defeated by their unnecessary deaths. But what else would count as a fantasy about justice in a community that had agreed on the legitimacy of its institutions?

For better or worse, a community can make its preordained victims bear the brunt of the crisis and solve its allocation decisions by letting its institutions do the choosing, but only when it has conferred legitimacy upon them. No wonder that Guido Calabresi (Calabresi and Babbitt 1978, p. 36) believes that allocation by responsible, accountable political institutions is unsatisfactory. This is the price of living in a plural society where legitimacy is always in doubt.

When individuals disagree on elementary justice, their most insoluble conflict is between institutions based on incompatible principles. The more severe the conflict, the more useful to understand the institutions that are doing most of the thinking. Exhortation will not help. Passing laws against discrimination will not help. It did not help African women for the League of Nations to pass resolutions against polygamy or female clitoridectomy. Preaching against wife battering and child abuse is not more likely to be effective than preaching against alcohol and drug abuse, racism, or sexism. Only changing institutions can help. We should address them, not individuals, and address them continuously, not only in crises.

So we should ask what happens to diplomacy when different kinds of institutions come into conflict. Between institutions of the same kind, based on the same analogies from nature, and sealed with the same ideas of justice, diplomacy has a chance. But diplomacy between different kinds of institutions will generally fail. Warnings will be misread. Appeals to nature and reason, compelling to one party, will seem childish or fraudulent to the other.

Once it were conceded that legitimated institutions make the big decisions, much else would be changed. Psychologists would not be able to claim that this extension of cognitive functions is a trivial matter, to be left unstudied in favor of children's unculturated perceptual and moral growth. Once it were conceded that the big decisions always engage ethical principles, then philosophers would not focus single-mindedly on individual moral dilemmas. Michael Sandel has written effectively against the bias that presents social theory with an unencumbered, unhistorical individual agent. He shows how theory supports self-contradiction for the sake of defending the premises of liberal philosophy (Sandel 1982). A theory of justice has to be balanced between theories of human agency, on the one hand, and theories of community on the other. If, in the theory of justice, the so-called community is of a kind that never penetrates the minds of its members, if their shared experiences within it make no difference to their wants and contribute nothing to their self-definition or to their ideas of merit, then much is wrong with the theory. Its conception of the self falls apart and its conception of the community is contradicted in the course of the argument. Sandel brings this criticism against John Rawls' *Theory of Justice* (1971), but it applies widely to many current discussions of justice, community, and self. Rawls describes two theories of community, both individualistic and neither sufficient to match the ordinary experience of human agency. And, after all, the premises of the principles of justice need to "bear *some* resemblance to the conditions of creatures discernibly human" (Sandel 1982, p. 43). In Rawls' first instrumental account of community, the subjects who cooperate are governed only by self-interested motivations, and the community good consists in their achieving their individual goals. On this account, community itself is external to their aims and interests. On Rawls' second account, the view that he adopts is called by Sandel the sentimental conception of community. It is partly internal to the subjects of cooperation, since it reaches their feelings. Both conceptions presuppose that the subject is individuated apart from or before the community experience, so the boundaries of the subject's selfhood are fixed independently of situations and are presumably incapable of change. Sandel, for his part, seeks a third conception by which the self would be profoundly penetrated by community, so that identity would even be constituted by it.

> On this strong view, to say that the members of a society are bound by a sense of community is not simply to say that a great many of them profess communitarian sentiments and pursue communitarian aims, but rather that they conceive their identity . . . as defined to some extent by the community of which they are a part. For them, community describes not just what they *have* as fellow citizens, but also what they *are*, not a relationship they choose (as in a voluntary association) but an attachment they discover, not merely an attribute but a constituent of their identity. In contrast to the instrumental and sentimental conceptions of community, we might describe this strong view as the constitutive conception. (Sandel 1982, p. 150)

The strong view requires a complete overhaul of vocabulary and a shift of assumptions. Instead of moral philosophy starting from a notion of the human subject as a sovereign agent for whom free choice is the essential condition, Sandel suggests that the human agent is essentially one who needs to discover (not choose) his ends, and that the community affords the means of self-discovery. Instead of being centered on the conditions of choice, a different kind of moral philosophy would be centered on the conditions of self-knowledge. To anyone who has been interested in Durkheim's theory of knowledge, this casts a comforting light.

Durkheim and Fleck taught that each kind of community is a thought world, expressed in its own thought style, penetrating the minds of its members, defining their experience, and setting the poles of their moral understanding. This program has always seemed raw and untried, needing too much work to make it acceptable. For all its insight and rightness, the trend against it seemed too strong. But Sandel gives the program back to past ages: being engaged in self-discovery, seeking in community to find his ends, is a human being "as the ancients conceived him" (Sandel 1982, p. 22). The tradition is old; these scenarios have been drawn before in literature and history. Only by deliberate bias and by an extraordinarily disciplined effort has it been possible to erect a theory of human behavior whose formal account of reasoning only considers the self-regarding motives, and a theory that has no possible way of including community-mindedness or altruism, still less heroism, except as an aberration. The Durkheim-Fleck program points to a way of return. For better or worse, individuals really do share their thoughts and they do to some extent harmonize their preferences, and they have no other way to make the big decisions except within the scope of institutions they build.

Bibliography

Abramson, A., et al., eds.
1974 *Critique of Anthropolgy,* An alternative journal published by graduate students of University College London: London: Bellers Press.

Arrow, Kenneth J.
1974 *The Limits of Organization,* from the Fels Lectures on public policy analysis. New York: Norton.
1984 *The Economics of Information.* Cambridge, Mass: Harvard University Press.

Bailey, Anne, and Joseph Llobera, eds.
1981 *The Asiatic Mode of Production.* London: Routledge & Kegan Paul.

Barber, Bernard
1961 "Resistance by Scientists to Scientific Discovery." *Science* 134 (3479): 596–602. Republished 1962 in *The Sociology of Science,* B. Barber and W. Hirsch, eds. New York: Free Press.

Barnes, John
1954 *Politics in a Changing Society: a Political History of the Fort Jameson Ngoni.* Oxford Unversity Press.

Barry, Brian
1978 "Circumstances of Justice and Future Generations." In *Obligations to Future Generations,* R. I. Sikora and B. Barry, eds. Philadelphia: Temple University Press.

Bartlett, Frederick
1923 *Psychology and Primitive Culture.* Cambridge University Press.

1927 *Psychology and the Soldier.* Cambridge University Press.

1932 *Remembering: an Experimental and Social Study.* Cambridge University Press.

1958 *Thinking.* New York: Basic Books.

Becker, Howard

1982 *Art Worlds.* Berkeley: University of California Press.

Black, Duncan

1948 "On the Rationale of Group Decision-Making." *Journal of Political Economy* 56(1):23–34.

Bloch, Maurice, ed.

1975 *Marxist Analyses and Social Anthropology.* London: Malaly Press.

Bloor, David

1976 *Knowledge and Social Imagery.* London: Routledge & Kegan Paul.

Bohannon, Laura

1952 "A Genealogical Charter." *Africa* 22(4): 301–15.

Boon, James A.

1977 *The Anthropological Romance of Bali, 1597–1972.* Cambridge University Press.

Broadbent, Donald E.

1970 Notice in *The Times,* London. Republished in *Dictionary of National Biography, 1961–70.* Oxford University Press. 1981.

Bulmer, Ralph

1967 "Why is the Cassowary not a Bird? A Problem of Zoological taxonomy among the Karam of the New Guinea Highlands." *Man* (N.S.)2:5–25.

Calabresi, Guido, and Philip Babbitt.

1978 *Tragic Choices.* New York: Norton.

Campbell, Donald

1975 "On the Conflicts Between Biological and Social Evolution and Between Psychology and Moral Tradition." *American Psychologist* 30(12):1103–26.

Chamberlin, John

1982 "Provision of Collective Goods as a Function of Group Size." In *Rational Man and Irrational Society?* B. Barry and R. Hardin, eds. London: Sage.

Christie, Agatha

1935 *The Labors of Hercules.* London: Greenway Edition.

Cohen, Stanley

1980 *Folks Devils and Moral Panics: the Creation of the Mods and the Rockers.* New York: St. Martin's Press.

Colby, Benjamin, and Michael Cole
   1973 "Culture, Memory and Narrative." *In Modes of Thought,* R. Horton and R. Finnegan, eds., 63–91. London: Faber & Faber.
Coleman, James, E. Katz, and H. Menzel,.
   1957 "The Diffusion of an Innovation among Physicians." *Sociometry* 20 (4): 253–70.
Condorcet, Jean Antoine Nicolas de Caritat, Marquis de
   1785 *Essai sur l'Application de l'Analyse à la probabilité des décisions rendues à la pluralité des voix.* Paris: Impr. Royale., Reprint, 1972. New York: Chelsea Publications.
Coser, Lewis
   1974 *Greedy Institutions: Patterns of Undivided Commitment.* New York: The Free Press.
Cunnison, I. G.
   1959 *The Luapula Peoples of Northern Rhodesia.* Manchester: University of Manchester Press.
De Soto, Clinton
   1960 "Learning a Social Structure." In *Social Networks, a Developing Paradigm,* S. Lienhardt, ed. New York: Academy Press, 1977.
Douglas, Mary
   1963 *The Lele of the Kasai.* International African Institute: Oxford University Press.
   1966 *Purity and Danger: an Analysis of Concepts of Pollution and Taboo.* London: Routledge & Kegan Paul.
   1970 "Deciphering a Meal" and "Self-evidence." In *Implicit Meanings.* London: Routledge & Kegan Paul, 1975.
   1973 *Rules and Meanings.* New York: Penguin.
   1980 *Evans-Pritchard.* Brighton: Harvester Press.
   1979 with Baron Isherwood. *The World of Goods.* New York: Basic Books.
   1986 *Risk Acceptability According to the Social Sciences.* New York: Basic Books.
   1982 with Aaron Wildavsky. *Risk and Culture.* Berkeley: University of California Press.
Dumont, Louis
   1966 *Homo Hierarchus: le Système des Castes et ses Implications.* Paris: Gallimard.
   1977 *Homo Aequalis: Génèse et Épanouisment de l'Idéologie Économique.* Paris: Gallimard.
   1983 *Essais sur l'Individualisme.* Paris: Du Seuil.
Durkheim, Emile.
   1893 *De la Division du Travail Social: Étude sur l'Organisation des Sociétés Supérieures.* Paris: Alcan. [Translation, 1933].

1895 *Les Règles de la Méthode Sociologique*. Paris: Alcan. [Translation, 1938].

1897 *Le Suicide: Ètude de Sociologie*. Paris: Alcan. [Translation, 1952].

1912 *Les Formes Élémentaries de la Vie Religieuse: le Système Totemique en Australie*. Paris: Alcan. [Translation, 1915].

1903 with M. Mauss, "De Quelques Formes Primitives de la Classification: Contribution à L'Ètude des Représentations Collectives." *L'Année Sociologique* 6:1–72.

Elster, Jon

1983 *Explaining Technical Change: a Case Study in the Philosophy of Science*. Cambridge University Press.

Evans-Pritchard, Edward

1940 *The Nuer: a Description of the Modes of Livelihood and Political Institutions of the Nilotic People*. Oxford: The Clarendon Press.

1951 *Kinship and Marriage among the Nuer*. Oxford: The Clarendon Press.

1956 *Nuer Religion*. Oxford: The Clarendon Press.

Festinger, Leon, D. Cartwright, K. Barber, J. Fleischl, J. Gottshanker, A. Keysen, and G. Leavitt

1948 "A Study of a Rumor: Its Origin and Spread." *Human Relations* 1(4): 464–86.

Firth, Raymond

1938 *Human Types*. Reprint, 1945 London: T. Nelson & Sons.

1940 *The Work of the Gods in Tikopia*. London: London School of Economics.

1968 Preface to *Kinship and Social Organization*, by W. H. R. Rivers. Reprint, 1914. London: Athlone Press.

Fitzgerald, Frances

1979 *America Revised: History Schoolbooks in the 20th Century*. Boston: Little, Brown.

Fleck, Ludwik

1935 *The Genesis and Development of a Scientific Fact*. Translation, 1979. Chicago: University of Chicago Press.

Fortes, Meyer, ed.

1949 *Social Structure: Studies Presented to A. R. Radcliffe-Brown*. Oxford Unversity Press.

Foucault, Michel

1970 *The Order of Things: an Archeology of the Human Sciences*. New York: Pantheon Books.

1976 *The History of Sexuality*. Translation, 1978. New York: Pantheon Books.

Fox, Renée, and Judith Swarez
> 1974 *The Courage to Fail: a Social View of Organ Transplants and Dialysis.* Chicago: University of Chicago Press.

Frazer, Sir James G.
> 1890 *The Golden Bough: a Study in Comparative Religion.* New York: Macmillan.

Friedman, Jonathan
> 1979 *System, Structure, and Contradiction in the Evolution of 'Asiatic' Social Formations.* Copenhagen: Nationalmuset.

Fuller, Lon
> 1949 "The Case of the Speluncean Explorers." *Harvard Law Review* 62: 616–45.

Gewirth, Alan
> 1978 *Reason and Morality.* Chicago: University of Chicago Press.

Ginsberg, Morris
> 1965 *On Justice in Society.* Ithaca, N.Y.: Cornell University Press.

Gluckman, Max
> 1941 "The Economy of the Central Barotse Plain." Rhodes-Livingston Paper no. 7. Manchester: Manchester University Press.
> 1947 "Malinowski's Functional Analysis of Social Change." *Africa* 16(4): 103–21.

Godelier, Maurice
> 1973 *Perspectives in Marxist Anthropology.* Translation, 1977. Cambridge University Press.

Goodman, Nelson
> 1972 *Problems and Projects.* Indianapolis, Ind.: Bobbs-Merrill.
> 1978 *Ways of Worldmaking.* Indianapolis, Ind.: Hackett Publishing.
> 1983 *Fact, Fiction and Forecast.* 4th ed. Cambridge, Mass.: Harvard University Press.

Gould, Stephen Jay
> 1981 *The Mismeasure of Man.* New York: Norton.

Greenwald, Anthony C.
> 1980 "The Totalitarian Ego: Fabrication and Revision of Personal History." *American Psychologist* 35 (7): 603–18.

Hacking, Ian
> 1982 "Language, Truth and Reason." *Rationality and Relativism.* Edited by Martin Hollis and Steven Lukes. Oxford: Blackwell.
> 1983 *Representing and Intervening: Introductory Topics in the Philosophy of Natural Science.* New York: Cambridge University Press.

1985 "Making Up People." In *Reconstructing Individualism*. In press. Stanford University Press.

Halbwachs, Maurice
1950 *La Mémoire Collective*. Paris: Presses Universitaires de France.

Hardin, Russell
1982 *Collective Action*. Baltimore: Johns Hopkins University Press.

Horton, R., and R. Finnegan, eds.
1973 *Modes of Thought: Essay on Thinking in Western and Non-Western Societies*. London: Faber & Faber.

Hume, David
1739 *A Treatise of Human Nature*. L.A. Selby-Bigge, ed. Rev. ed., 1958. Oxford: The Clarendon Press.
1751 *An Inquiry Concerning the Principles of Morals*. Rev. ed., 1957. New York: Liberal Arts Press.
1777 *Enquiries Concerning Human Understanding and Concerning the Principles of Morals*. Rev. ed., 1975. Oxford: The Clarendon Press.

James, William
1890 *The Principles of Psychology*. 2 vols. Reprint 1962, New York: Smith.

Jaspers, J. M. F., and C. Frazer
1981 "Attitudes and Social Representations." Chapter 10 in *Social Representations*, S. Moscovici and R. Farr, eds. Cambridge University Press.

Jayyusi, Lena
1984 *Categorization and the Moral Order*. London: Routledge & Kegan Paul.

Jevons, W. S.
1874 *The Principles of Science, A Treatise on Logic and Scientific Method*. 3rd ed., 1879. London: Macmillan.

Johnson, Hugh, ed.
1985 *World Atlas of Wine*. United Kingdom: RHS Entrprises.

Kaberry, Phyllis
1952 *Women of the Grassfields; a Study of the Economic Position of Women in Bamenda, British Cameroons*. London: H.M. Stationary Office.

Khare, R. S.
1985 *Culture and Democracy: Anthropological Reflections on Modern India*. Lanham, Md.: University Press of America.

Klein, Melanie.
1975 *Envy and Gratitude and Other Works, 1946–1963*. London: Hogarth Press.

Kuhn, Thomas
1962 *The Structure of Scientific Revolutions*. Chicago: University of

Chicago Press.

1979 Introduction to *The Genesis and Development of a Scientific Fact* by Ludwik Fleck. Chicago: University of Chicago Press.

Landau, Martin

1973 "On the Concept of a Self-Correcting Organization." *Public Administration Review* 33(6): 533–42.

Lee, Richard, and Irven DeVore, eds.

1968 *Man the Hunter.* Chicago: Wenner-Grenn Foundation.

Lévi-Strauss, Claude

1962 [1966] *The Savage Mind.* Translation, 1962. London: Weidenfeld and Nicolson.

1963 "The Bear and the Barber." *Journal of the Royal Anthropological Institute* 93 (1): 1–11.

1984 *The View From Afar.* New York: Basic Books.

Lewin, Bernard

1969 *The Image and the Past.* New York: International Universities Press.

Lewis, David

1968 *Convention: A Philosophical Study.* Cambridge, Mass.: Harvard University Press.

Lloyd, Geoffrey E. R.

1966 *Polarity and Analogy: Two Types of Argumentation in Early Greek Thought.* Cambridge: Cambridge University Press.

Macbeath, Alexander

1952 *Experiments in Living; a Study of the Nature and Foundations of Ethics or Morals in the Light of Recent Work in Social Anthropology.* London: Macmillan.

MacIntyre, Alasdair

1981 *After Virtue: a Study in Moral Theory.* University of Notre Dame Press.

Mackenzie, Donald

1980 *Statistics in Britain, 1865–1930: the Sociological Construction of Scientific Knowledge.* Edinburgh University Press.

Medin, Douglas and Murphy, G. L.

1985 "The Role of Theories in Conceptual Coherence." *Psychological Review* 92(3): 289–315.

Meillassoux, Claude

1981 *Maidens, Meal and Money: Capitalism and the Domestic Community.* Cambridge University Press.

Merton, Robert K.

1949 "The Self-Fulfilling Prophecy." In *Social Theory and Social Structure* 475–90. 1968. New York: The Free Press.

1957 "Priorities in Scientific Discovery: a Chapter in the Sociology of Science." *American Sociological Review* 22(6): 635–59.

1962 "Singletons and Multiples in Scientific Discovery: a Chapter in the Sociology of Science." *Proceedings of the American Philosophical Society* 105(5): 471–87.

1963 "Resistance to the Study of Multiple Discoveries in Science." *European Journal of Sociology* (Archives) 4(2): 237–82.

1965 *On the Shoulders of Giants: a Shandean Postscript.* New York: Harcourt, Brace.

Mill, James
1869 *Analysis of the Phenomena of the Human Mind.* Reprint, 1982. New York: Hildesheim.

Mill, John Stuart
1888 *A System of Logic: Ratiocinative and Inductive.* Reprint, 1967. London: Longmans, Green & Co.

Miller, David
1976 *Social Justice.* Oxford: The Clarendon Press.

Myers, C. S.
1911 *A Textbook of Experimental Psychology.* London: Longmans.

Needham, Rodney
1973 *Right and Left, Essays on Dual Classification.* Chicago: University of Chicago Press.

Nelkin, Dorothy
1977 *Science Textbook Controversies and the Politics of Equal Time.* Cambridge University Press.

Nelson, Benjamin
1981 *On the Roads to Modernity: Conscience, Science and Civilizations: Selected Writings,* Toby Huff, ed. New Jersey: Rowman & Littlefield.

Nielsen, Kai
1984 "Against Ethical Rationalism." A chapter in *Gewirth's Ethical Rationalism,* E. Regis Jr., ed. Chicago: University of Chicago Press.

O'Flaherty, Wendy
1984 *Dreams, Illusions and Other Realities.* Chicago: University of Chicago Press.

Olson, Mancur
1965 *The Logic of Collective Action: Public Goods and the Theory of Groups.* Cambridge, Mass.: Harvard University Press.

Perkin, Harold
1969 *Origins of Modern English Society, 1780–1880.* London: Routledge & Kegan Paul.

Prigogine, Ilya
1980 *From Being to Becoming: Time and Complexity in the Physical Sciences.* San Francisco: W. H. Freeman.

Quine, W. V.
    1961 *From a Logical Point of View*, New York: Harper & Row.
    1969 *Ontological Relativity and Other Essays*. New York: Columbia University Press.

Radcliffe-Brown, A. R.
    1945 "Religion and Society." In *Structure and Function in Primitive Society*. London: Cohen & West, Ltd.

Rathje, William, G. G. Harrison, W. Hughes
    1975 "Food Waste Behavior in an Urban Population." *Journal of Nutrition Education* 7(1):13–16. Oakland, Ca.: Society for Nutrition Education.

Rawls, John
    1971 *A Theory of Justice*. Cambridge, Mass.: Belknap, Harvard University Press.

Rayner, Steve
    1982 "The Perception of Time and Space in Egalitarian Sects: a Millenarian Cosmology." In *Essays in the Sociology of Perception*, M. Douglas, ed. London: Routledge & Kegan Paul.

Reddy, William
    1986 "The Structure of a Cultural Crisis: Thinking about Cloth before and after the Revolution." In *Commodities and Culture: the Social Life of Things*, A. Appadurai, ed. Cambridge University Press.

Rivers, W. H. R.
    1908 "A Human Experiment in Nerve Division." *Brain* 31:323–450.
    1918 *Dreams and Primitive Culture*. 2d ed., 1922. Cambridge University Press.
    1920 *Instinct and the Unconscious: a Contribution to a Biological Theory of the Psycho-Neuroses*. Reprint, 1922. Cambridge University Press.

Rosen, Lawrence
    1984 *Bargaining for Reality: the Construction of Social Relations in a Muslim Community*. Chicago: University of Chicago Press.

Sahlins, Marshall
    1972 *Stone Age Economics*. London: Tavistock.
    1976 *Culture and Practical Reason*. Chicago: University of Chicago Press.

Sandel, Michael
    1982 *Liberalism and the Limits of Justice*. Cambridge University Press.

Schelling, Thomas
    1960 *The Strategy of Conflict*. New York: Oxford University Press.
    1978 *Micromotives and Macrobehavior*. New York: Norton.

Schotter, Andrew
     1981 *The Economic Theory of Social Institutions.* Cambridge Univer-
          sity Press.
Selby-Bigge. L. A.
     1893 Introduction to *An Enquiry Concerning Human Understanding
          and Concerning the Principles of Morals* by David Hume [1777].
          3d ed., 1975. Oxford: The Clarendon Press.
Sen, Amartya
     1981 *Poverty and Famines: an Essay on Entitlement and Deprivation.*
          Oxford: The Clarendon Press.
Service, Elman
     1966 *The Hunters.* [Reprint, 1977] Englewood Cliffs, N.J.: Prentice-
          Hall.
Shapin, S., and B. Barnes
     1976 "Head and Hand: Rhetorical Resources in British Pedagogical
          Writing, 1770–1850." *Oxford Review of Education* 2(3): 231–54.
Simon, Herbert
     1955 "A Behavioral Model of Rational Choice." In *Models of Thought.*
          New Haven: Yale University Press.
Smith, V. Kerry
     1984 "A Theoretical Analysis of the 'Green Lobby'." *The American
          Political Science Review* 79: 132–47.
Stinchcombe, Arthur
     1968 *Constructing Social Theories.* New York: Harcourt, Brace &
          World.
Strathern, Marilyn
     1980 *Nature, Culture and Gender.* Cambridge University Press.
Tambiah, S. J.
     1969 "Animals are Good to Think and Good to Prohibit." *Ethnology*
          8(4): 424–59.
Taylor, Michael
     1982 *Community, Anarchy and Liberty.* Cambridge University Press.
Terray, Emmanuel
     1969 *Marxism and "Primitive" Societies.* Translation, 1972. New
          York: Monthly Review Press.
Torry, William
     1984 "Morality and Harm: Hindu Peasant Adjustments to Famines."
          Forthcoming, 1986, in *Social Science Information.*
Trenn, Thaddeus J.
     1979 Preface to *Genesis and Development of a Scientific Fact* by Lud-
          wik Fleck. Chicago: University of Chicago Press.

Ward, James
1920 *Psychological Principles*. Cambridge University Press.

Weber, Max
1905 *The Protestant Ethic and the Spirit of Capitalism*. 1930. New York: Scribners.

Williamson, Oliver E.
1975 *Markets and Hierarchies: Analysis and Anti-Trust Implications, a Study in the Economics of Internal Organization*. New York: Free Press.

Yalow, Rosalyn
1985 "Radioactivity in the Service of Humanity." *Fordham University Quarterly* 60(236): 5–17.

Index

Abramson, A., 28
Altruism, 11, 21, 31, 128
Anarchy, 29
Ancestor worship, 35–37, 50–53
L'Année Sociologique, 70, 86
Anomie, 97–98
Anthropology, x, 17, 27, 34, 67; folk classification and, 57–59; functionalism and, 39, 42–43, 48; social, 70–71
Arendt, Hannah, x
Arrow, Kenneth J., 46; Impossibility Theorem of, 77–79
Attitude research, 82
Authority, 13

Babbitt, Philip, 125
Bacon, Francis, 70–71
Bailey, Anne, 28
Barnes, B., 49
Barry, Brian, 117–19, 125
Bartlett, Frederick, 71, 81; conventionalization and, 83–84, 87–88; experimental designs and, 88–89; Haddon and, 83–84, 87–88; memory and, 87–89; perception theory and,

83–89; Rivers and, 83–90; social/individual development and, 86–90
Becker, Howard, 16
Benthamism, 10, 79–80
Black, Duncan, 78–79
Bloch, Maurice, 28
Bloor, David, 59
Boon, James A., 115
Bricolage, 66–67
British Journal of Psychology, 83
Broadbent, Donald E., 88

Calabresi, Guido, 125
Cambridge Psychology Laboratory, 83
Campbell, Donald, 82–83
Causality, 11–12. *See also* David Hume
Censorship, 85
Chamberlin, John, 24
Christie, Agatha, 114
Classification: behavior and, 100–102, 108–109; dichotomous, 56–57; "fit" and, 17, 97–98; folk v. scientific, 56–59; institutions and, 3, 48–49, 55, 63–67, 91–109, 112; naming and, 100–109, 112; purposes of, 100; sameness and, 53, 55–63; textiles,

141

HOW INSTITUTIONS THINK

was composed in 10-point Mergenthaler Linotron 202 Aster and leaded 2 points
by Coghill Book Typesetting Co.;
with ornaments provided by Job Litho Services;
printed sheet-fed offset on 50-pound, acid-free Glatfelter B-31,
Smyth sewn and bound over 80-point binder's boards in Holliston Roxite B,
also adhesive bound with paper covers by Thomson-Shore, Inc.;
with dust jackets and paper covers printed in 2 colors by Philips Offset Company, Inc.;
and published by

SYRACUSE UNIVERSITY PRESS

SYRACUSE, NEW YORK 13244-5160